Marlia Cochran never ceases to amaze me! *Where is My White Picket Fence?* is a book nearly every woman can identify with. We have all struggled with being a "good girl" on some level. This is a must read for any woman who longs for joy in their life!

Terilee Harrison
Author, Speaker, Radio Show Co-Host
www.TerileeHarrison.com

What Readers are Saying....

Marlia's raw transparency shone a light in the hidden recesses of my heart...exposing the pain of my own "white picket fence" expectations and allowing me to bring truth to lies I didn't even know I believed. Her journey created a path and a process that I can now walk on a daily basis – every time unfulfilled expectations steal my joy and peace. This is one book I will be recommending during my coaching sessions for years to come!

Pastor Tami (aka "The Ledge Coach")
Founder of Pastor Tami Ministries
and HungryHearts4God.com, Transformational Messenger,
and Author of *Glory to Glory: The Tale of a Hungry Heart*

Having come through my own life-challenging experience, Marlia's story resonated with me on so many levels. Mainly, I felt completely disillusioned, as if my joy had been stolen from me and replaced with feelings of betrayal, fraud, imperfection, and fear. I didn't want anyone to know my frailties and sunk deep into my own reclusiveness. Marlia's story revealed how un-alone I was, how mistaken my thinking was, and that again, Father God is always here to love, nurture, and protect us only as *we* will allow.

Renée E. Cabourne, CFP®
Money Savvy Woman

Marlia opens the emotional floodgates with her story and reveals such powerful truths about the disillusionment of being society's "good girl" and the painful traps of perfectionism. She is so raw, honest, and relatable. An amazing read if you want to strengthen your personal relationship with God and learn to walk in joy.

Jenee Dana
My Focus Book

Where's My White Picket Fence?

When a Good Girl Doubts God

by

Marlia C. Cochran

Where's My White Picket Fence?

When a Good Girl Doubts God

Published by
Good Girl Enterprises
Upland, California

www.GoodGirlEnterprises.com

Cover Design by Dan Mulhern Design
Interior Design by Dawn Teagarden

ISBN: 978-0-9890884-0-4

Printed in the United States of America

www.GoodGirlEnterprises.com

*To all the good girls, especially to the one that
birthed me and the one that I birthed…
may you always walk in the true joy
that our Good Father has promised.*

*In loving memory of my Dad, Clint Correll,
and my Mom-In-Love, Barbara Cochran*

Acknowledgments

Six years ago, I started telling people that I was writing a book. What I was actually doing was rewriting the same introductory sentence over and over again, and yet these people wouldn't let me give up, wouldn't let me settle, wouldn't let me continue to not fulfill my calling. They supported me in various ways, each different, but all so very necessary…and for that, I owe them an immeasurable amount of love and gratitude.

To my Good and Gracious Heavenly Daddy, who patiently and persistently waited for me to see the real You and how much You truly love me. Thank You for never giving up on me, or what You called me to and destined me for, but for pursuing me all the way. Thank You, most of all, for sending Your Son Jesus to die on a cross so that I might have a relationship with You, filled with Your saving grace and redemption. Thank You also for blessing me with Your Holy Spirit, who truly has been my Great Comforter and Teacher.

To My family

Josh, My Love, you are the man who has fully demonstrated the grace, mercy, and unconditional love of God by how you have loved, honored, and cherished me. I am amazed at how much we have experienced, and how even the bumps and bruises along the way have only made our relationship and love even stronger. Thank you so much for your support, and for never letting me give up on writing this book…even though I wanted to so many times. Your belief in me carried me when I couldn't believe in myself. You are my best friend, the love of my life, the one that I can't wait to spend the rest of my life with… "Place me like a seal over you heart, like a seal on your arm; for love is as strong as death…"

My Sweetest Sweetness, Savannah Charis, just as the meaning of your name, you truly have been God's gracious gift in the desert for me – a greater blessing than I could have ever imagined. You never fail to keep me on my toes with your busy curiosity and sweet yet spunky disposition that continues to play out in different ways as you grow up way too fast before me. Your love and gentle compassion, that so naturally flows out of you, challenges me to be the same. And because of all of this, and so much more, you are the reason I knew there must really be a Good Father who wanted to give us joy, and have so fervently pursued it. My prayer for you is that you will always know, and never have to doubt, how much God loves you and the amazing call He placed on your life the very day you were conceived. I pray that you will always be certain of my unconditional love for you and that regardless of what journey you walk in this life, your mama will always have your back. "You are my sweetness, my grace and God's gift, Savannah, Savannah, Savannah Charis."

To Mom, for always being my #1 fan and encouraging me in the pursuit of everything God has called me to, even when others doubted. Thank you for helping me when I couldn't help myself and faithfully praying me out of the darkest time of my life. You were always a great mom, but you've also become a great friend.

We'll always have Italy…and who knows what else! I love you.

To Dad, who showed me what generosity and selfless service to God really looks like. Your love of serving the youth and leading them to the feet of Jesus through the years helped to ignite my own passion for them. Thank you for being a man of God who demonstrated love and commitment to your family, even when it wasn't easy. Even though I know I'll see you again, I miss you here more and more every day.

To Barb, you were the best mom-in-love a girl could ever have. Thank you for not only making me always feel like a daughter, but also your friend. Thank you, even more, for helping me to know how to love your boy in a way like you loved his dad. You were an amazing woman of God, and I miss and love you more than words could express.

To Mike, the other half of the best parents-in-love that I could have ever been blessed with. You are a gentle warrior who has been a rock for us more times than I can count. Thank you for also being my dad-away-from-dad and loving me like one of your own. I am so blessed by you and the example of a Godly husband and dad that you have always been. Now, tell me a joke…I promise I'll laugh!

To my brothers and sisters, (by blood and marriage!), for every different way that you have loved and supported me throughout the years. You each continually amaze me in your strength and perseverance. I love you!

To my nieces and nephews, this book is also written for each of you. You will walk your own journey, experience your own highs and lows, but my prayer is that in all of it, you will hold tightly to your relationship with Jesus. That in the midst of whatever you may find yourself, that you will be able to authentically say you have the "joy of the Lord." I look at each of you and know that God has His hand on your lives and that you have each been called for a specific purpose...and it will be amazing! I love you so, so much.

To My Friends

To the ladies (and gents!) who have stuck with me through everything, the good and the bad. You have been my support system, my sounding board, and my accountability. You have been the ones to make me laugh, and sit with me while I cry and process through the deep questions of faith and life. Thank you for truly being a second family...I love each of you.

To My Mentors, Teachers, and Spiritual Leaders...

To Pastors Rick and Janet MacDonald and the whole AZHOP family. You have given us a space for true spiritual healing and shown us a deep, abiding love that we so needed. You have helped us to discover amazing gifts and witness awesome miracles. You have stood with us, fasted for us, and prayed over us, helping us to see what the Body of Christ is all about. We love you...you will always be home.

To Dr. Gordon Coulter, who walked with me through my education and gave me my first chance at the "big leagues" of academia. But even more, you believed in me and helped me to gain the confidence as a woman in leadership that had eluded me for so long. Thank you for being more than just a mentor, but also a spiritual dad to me. I wish that we could have had more time…I have so many more questions.

To Karla Franko, my spiritual mom, who I called crazy at first but wouldn't let me leave God in a box. You introduced me to the power of the Holy Spirit and blew that box and my logical mind wide open. You were such a divine appointment that I thank God for constantly. You helped to heal lies and gave me a place to practice and explore all that the Holy Spirit gifted me with. We have got do Acts 2 again someday!

To Pastor Vern Burgess, who started it all. If you hadn't challenged me at such an early age to walk in the anointing that God had placed on me, who knows where I would be. You were an amazing youth pastor that gave me the chance to test out the waters, mistakes and all.

To The Ones Who Helped Bring Me Back to Life…Literally

Dr. Lamioko Pappoe, Dr. Jaffar Tremazi, Dr. Jayapal Reddy, and Dr. Elbert Chang, because you were all part of the miracle of saving my life. Thank you for being willing to look at more than the test results and statistics, and for seeing me as more than just a file. You have helped me to walk the long road back to my new normal, and for that, I can never thank you enough.

To Visalus Sciences, aka Body By Vi, you have been an absolute miracle sent by God Himself! Because of your commitment to excellence and purity of product, I was finally able to lose the weight required for me to be placed on the kidney transplant list. Thank you for helping me get back to a place of normalcy as a wife and mom that I hadn't experienced in years. I finally have the energy my busy life requires! Truly a priceless gift…"Thank You" will never be enough!

To The Cocoon

You spent months, Tuesday after Tuesday, making it safe for me to process through years of disillusionment, asking me the questions that would lead me to the deepest places of fear and uncertainty that needed to be uprooted for my healing as well as for the readers'. Thank you for modeling to me what real authenticity and transparency looks like and then holding me accountable to do the same. You are such phenomenal women who have been a blessing from God, and I'm so grateful for each of you.

To the production team…oh my gosh, you guys are phenomenal!!! Every aspect of the book and getting it complete was made so much easier because of each of you. Thanks for being miracle workers!

And last, but certainly not least, to the amazing Amanda Johnson, my fearless book coach who has become my friend. It wasn't a coincidence that I saw Jenee's post on Facebook that day touting how awesome her book coach was, and that God had been pressing me to get one myself. However, I'm pretty sure that if I had known when I started, what these past 18 months would entail, I would have surely chickened out because I was never planning on actually writing my story. But you knew, and you wouldn't let me settle for less than what God wanted to redeem in me. Thank you for not letting me give up, but instead helping me to work past just inspirational to something that is transformational... And to think, all I wanted to do was write a flippin' book! You have truly been a gift from God!

Contents

Introduction

———————— ⌘⌘⌘ ————————

The word of the LORD came to me, saying,
"Before I formed you in the womb I knew you,
before you were born I set you apart;
I appointed you as a prophet to the nations."

"Alas, Sovereign LORD," I said, "I do not know
how to speak; I am too young."

But the LORD said to me, "Do not say, 'I am
too young.' You must go to everyone I send
you to and say whatever I command you. Do
not be afraid of them, for I am with you and
will rescue you," declares the LORD.

Then the LORD reached out his hand and
touched my mouth and said to me, "I have put
my words in your mouth. See, today I appoint
you over nations and kingdoms to uproot and
tear down, to destroy and overthrow,
to build and to plant."

—Jeremiah 1:4-10 (NIV version)

———————— ⌘⌘⌘ ————————

I sat at my computer, reviewing the pictures that my radio co-host and I had taken for our website. Feeling pressure to decide which one I liked most, I struggled to nail it down.

"Hey, Josh! Can you help me choose a picture, please? I can't figure out which one will go best with our page layout."

"Sure, Babe. Too many good ones, huh?"

"Yeah, they are pretty good." It was the first time in years that I hadn't completely hated a picture of myself.

I scooted over so that he could squeeze in another chair for himself. He took over the mouse and started scrolling through them, one by one. At first, he went kind of fast, but the more he looked at them, the slower he scrolled, until he finally stopped on one and stared.

I finally broke the silence, "Well, what do you think?"

He seemed to be lost in thought for a moment, and then he looked up, teary-eyed, "Do you see it?"

Puzzled, I responded, "See what?" I leaned closer to see what he was referring to.

"Mar, it looks like the old you — the *real* you. Look at your eyes... how different. You seem so young...so light...so...free."

Wow, I do look different. The light is back in my eyes. It actually looks like joy peeking through!

I put my hand in his before looking in his eyes and saying something I'm sure he never thought he would hear after the last decade we had walked together, "Josh, I have a feeling that this is just the beginning…"

Later that evening, as Josh put our daughter to bed, I tried to think back to the last time I looked like that…happy…joyful.

When I had Savannah? Our wedding day?

I attempted to track through my memory for other specific moments or time periods, but they just weren't there.

Wow, it really has been years!

And then another disturbing thought surfaced.

Even in those circumstances, was it really joy? Did I even know how to have joy then?

What happened? That was the question that wracked my brain.

How was it that I was a young woman, living with an amazing husband and a beautiful daughter, and still couldn't find joy. I spent years in seminary and left with two (almost three) degrees, committed my life to studying the Word of God, and still didn't know what joy was.

I should've known how to experience the joy God promised me. I should've known how to bring it into my home, walk it in my marriage, raise my daughter up in it…feel it in my heart. What happened?!?!

Feeling abandoned, escaping a crazy boyfriend, running away from a difficult ministry, having a special needs child, an insane illness, and a horrible brush with death...that is what happened.

Of course, I hadn't been happy.

No one had prepared me for all of the loss and pain. Big or small, the tragedy didn't matter anymore. I just got used to being constantly disappointed by life.

Where is my white picket fence, God?

Over the years, I'd really done my best — well, most of the time — to hang on to some hope that there was a point for all of the crazy experiences I'd had in just three decades of life. I had read the scripture "**that in all things, God works for the good of those who love Him**" but I didn't see it happening in my life. In fact, for a few years there, it was just one insane crisis after another.

Where is God in all of this?

I had also done my best to maintain some composure and semblance of control. After all, I was a youth pastor, serving families. And I did whatever I could to induce the joy.

> *No one had prepared me for all of the loss and pain. Big or small, the tragedy didn't matter anymore. I just got used to being constantly disappointed by my life.*

I tried to please my parents, and I tried to please God. I tried to be the Good Girl. I earned almost three degrees. I served until my bones were tired. Nothing worked. Not losing weight. Not building a successful business as an entrepreneur. Not ambitiously running from network meeting to network meeting so everyone knew who I was. Nothing. But I kept thinking with every task, with every pursuit, with every accomplishment, *I know I'll be happy when...* only to realize that it left me emptier than before and desperately craving something more. Something deeper. Something life-changing.

It wasn't until God prompted me to write a book two years ago that things began to shift in a new direction, and it didn't exactly feel like a good direction at first. I finally gave in to the strong sense that had started before my early twenties — that God was preparing me to write a book. I thought it was going to be a book about youth ministry...maybe even about women in leadership ministry.

However, after all of the life experience, I felt called to write a book to help women deal with disillusionment. I found a book coach and enlisted her help, and we both realized about the same time that the journey was not going to look anything like I'd imagined. In fact, I couldn't have been more wrong.

Never, in my wildest dreams, would I have imagined that it would be a story so vulnerable, so raw, and so intimate that it would take me two years to make it permanent on paper. Never did I think the process would be so transformational.

But it has been. That's what my husband saw in the picture. That's what the community that has walked with me for two years has reflected back to me. And that is what I now see in the mirror…a transformed woman who has found what she always craved — Joy.

I have to tell you the truth. I never wanted to tell *my* story, and I didn't think it was required to help other women, but looking back on the journey I've walked, I've come to realize that the raw stories would have really helped me during that dark time. If I could have just seen someone else telling the truth about how they felt and what they did while walking the journey, maybe something would have clicked. Maybe I could have somehow walked with them and learned. I had the truth in my head (God promised me joy!), but it hadn't made its way to my heart and into my life yet.

We all have the truth in our heads. We know the Bible verses. We know what we have been taught. We even know the right steps to take.

So, what is it? What's missing? What keeps us stuck in disillusionment?

We know the Bible verses. We know what we have been taught. We even know the right steps to take. So, what's missing? What keeps us stuck in disillusionment?

My prayer is that you find the answer to that question in the pages of my story — that you are inspired to see the steps, the practices, and the tools that God has for you in here.

I didn't always believe it myself. But it's true. Joy is real. It's possible. And…it's a journey.

May you find your joy!

Marlia

Chapter 1

Where's My White Picket Fence?

I am the man who has seen affliction
by the rod of the LORD's wrath.
He has driven me away and made me walk
in darkness rather than light; indeed,
he has turned his hand against me
again and again, all day long.
He has made my skin and my flesh grow old
and has broken my bones.
He has besieged me and surrounded me
with bitterness and hardship.
He has made me dwell in darkness
like those long dead.
He has walled me in so I cannot escape;
he has weighed me down with chains.
Even when I call out or cry for help,
he shuts out my prayer.
He has barred my way with blocks of stone;
he has made my paths crooked.

-Lamentations 3:1 - 9

The steamy water bubbled up around me like lava as I gingerly slipped my body into our backyard hot tub. As I sank in, I hardly noticed the beaming sun, the soft breeze that blew across my shoulders, and the flowers that were beginning to wake from their wintery nap. My sole aim was to completely submerge into the only thing that gave me any sort of relief from the constant and near maddening ache that consumed every joint that held me together.

God, where are you?!? How could you leave me in this, like this?

I hadn't lived a perfect life, but I had tried to do the right things, to be a good girl.

This is what I get? Don't good girls get good things?

Don't good girls get the life they dreamed of? You know, the one with their Prince Charming and cherubic babies all sitting on the porch swing of their big perfect house with the immaculate yard and white picket fence?

Where is MY white picket fence?

At least that's what I had been led to believe my whole life by my parents, family, and church. All I could feel was an all-consuming bitterness towards God for what seemed like the ultimate double-crossing at a time that I needed Him the most.

Not only is my body betraying me, but so is my God. If this is how You are going to play, I am done with Your game.

I wanted nothing more to do with a so-called "good and faithful Father," because how could a good father do this to His daughter,

His princess, His favorite?

In Search Of My Missing Fence

When I was a little girl, I had dreams of my perfect life. I was going to be married to a good, strong man, and we were going to be extremely *happy* and hardly ever fight. I was going to have a bunch of healthy, *happy* babies with him and really enjoy being a mom. And of course, my children were going to grow up and change the world. We were going to live in a big, beautiful home, with a wrap around porch surrounded by a white picket fence and a neighborhood full of friends and family we could comfortably call confidants and cheerleaders. We would all be healthy and *happy* and live a picturesque life...*happily* ever after.

> *We would all be healthy and happy and live a picturesque life... happily ever after.*

Sure, my white picket fence dream was influenced by fairy tales, but it was also influenced by *Better Home & Garden* magazines and *The Martha Stewart Show*.

Over the years, my white picket fence dream also included ministry. When I was 13 years old, I was clear that God had placed a specific call on my life to reach the youth culture. I knew that it wouldn't be easy, but I did have a sense, and expectation, that He would make the path smooth.

But something had happened to my white picket fence. Somewhere along the line, the fence started to fall apart, disintegrate, and disappear completely.

One white piece of wood after another came crashing down with every broken dream, and I found myself asking, "God, where's *my* white picket fence?"

And the disillusionment set in.

I slowly reached for my daily companion, an oversized black golf umbrella, and popped it open over my head. Even though the original reason for it was to protect my sensitive skin from the sun, it had become more than just a shield from the sun. I pulled it down, letting the pointed tips touch the water and create a cave as I sank up to my neck, completely cutting myself off from everything but my misery and seething rage.

How could You betray me? Haven't I done enough for You? I've given up everything for You, dedicated my life to You! I've been underpaid and undervalued, all in the name of serving You, and THIS is what I get?!?

Shifting in discomfort and trying to find a position that would relieve the constant throbbing, a greater pain pounded across my memory.

Goodbye, Ministry

I sat on the front steps of our house, phone dangling loosely in my hand, stunned at the unexpected conversation I had just finished. Tears streaming down my face, I repeatedly replayed it in my mind, trying to figure out where it had gone sideways.

"I am so disappointed in you."

His voice was harsh and biting, as the worst words that anyone could say to me just hung in the air. I didn't quite know how to respond, but I knew that what I wanted to do most was burst into tears.

> *"I am so disappointed in you." His voice was harsh and biting...*

I was determined, however, not to let him hear that it hurt me, cutting deeply into my already broken spirit, and so I pleadingly replied, "What do you want me to do then?"

Sharply, he said, "It doesn't really matter at this point. I'm just so disappointed."

The rest of the conversation just faded away because it was completely inconsequential at that point. It didn't matter that what disappointed him was out of my control and really was not even about me to begin with, but just the fact that he said those words to me was a knife to my heart.

My chest tightened with an overwhelming sense of confusion and sadness at what our relationship had come to. He was my boss, my pastor, my mentor, a father figure, and a man that I had greatly admired for many years. The last couple of them, however, had been extremely difficult in our working relationship. And unfortunately, it often times played out in staff meetings as our wills clashed. He said things that cut to the core of me, and I would sulk in the corner. What it really came down to is that after years of training and mentoring, I was ready to try out my wings, but he didn't seem ready for me to take a bigger role, or maybe he was afraid I would leave the nest.

With my head hung forward, the tears continued to flow into little droplet marks on the concrete stairs, and my heart felt the stabbing ache of the inevitable. As much as I loved the man, it felt like I had sustained a mortal spiritual wound over the last few years, and I wasn't sure if I could forgive him for all of it, or even how much longer I could keep trying.

I gotta get out of here. The nest, the ministry, all of it.

What about My Daughter?

Long before I became sick, I was visiting doctors, not for myself, but for my sweet little two-year-old Savannah. We had gone to doctor after doctor, trying to find the answer as to why my beautiful baby girl had suffered with upwards of 60 seizures a day since she was five months old.

I now sat across from another white coat, with my little dark-haired angel playing at my feet, wishing that I had Josh's hand to stabilize me. This was the one and only appointment he had ever missed, and I had a strange feeling that this might be the most important so far.

―❦―

"Your daughter has a condition called micro-cephaly..."

―❦―

The doctor rustled the papers and then looked up with a gentle smile, "The tests came back conclusive, which will give us a place to launch from for treatment."

Okay, okay, don't drag this out, Just come on with it already!

"Your daughter has a condition called microcephaly, which means that she was born with a very small head, and it has never grown to typical size. Since she's only maintained a standing of being in the two percentile on the growth chart for her head circumference, this would be the reason for her seizures."

"So it's not epilepsy? That's good, right?" Savannah grabbed onto my hand and began kissing it with her sweet pink lips. I smiled down at her and then back at her neurologist.

"No, it's not epilepsy. However, you need to understand that because of the severity of her past seizures and the fact that her head may never get any bigger, she will have extreme delays, as she is already displaying."

I can't stop smiling, Why can't I stop smiling?

"Her speech will more than likely not increase past very basic. She will have great difficulty with her gross motor skills like walking and running as well as her fine motor skills. She will probably never be in a typical classroom because of the extreme learning delays. And there is a chance that she could become quadriplegic." I could feel myself nod my head slowly up and down with that stupid smile still on my face. "I will recommend an aggressive treatment and therapy so that we might have a chance at some functionality, but this is going to be a long, hard road for her…and you."

As I gathered up her toys and shoved them into her diaper bag, I looked at my baby and couldn't understand how something so beautiful and perfect could have such a devastating future. The doctor said he would set up the next appointment as he tweaked Savannah's nose and provoked a giggle.

God, how did this happen? Why did this happen? What did I do? Why are you punishing her for my screw-ups?

I cringed in agony as the memories radiated into the depths of my bones. Most mornings, I sat quietly under my black umbrella while brooding and boiling on the inside at what my life had become. *Useless and desperate.* Other mornings, however, were much worse. I would scream at the top of my lungs, trying to reach the God I felt had abandoned me. I threw accusations of betrayal and hatred, questioning everything I thought I knew about Him. This was one of those mornings.

Ten years of ministry, two degrees, and a world of heartache…You owe me, us, something more than this! You say you're a good Father who only gives good gifts, but this isn't good and you're nothing but a liar!

My Black Umbrella

The loss of my white picket fence overwhelmed me. I didn't understand how God could leave me hanging, especially when I had devoted my entire life to Him. I didn't know what else to do except hang on to that black umbrella, and all of my anger, disillusionment, and tantrum.

Good girls get good things, not mysterious illnesses that keep them from playing with their baby girl! I was supposed to have a happy, healthy baby, and be happy and healthy myself. What happened? Where are you?

My expectations of the way my life was supposed to be hung heavy over me, and just like that big black umbrella I held over my head, they caused me to walk under a darkness that eventually affected every aspect of our lives.

I may have put the physical black umbrella down when I got out of the hot tub every day, but I took the anger, bitterness, and pain back into the house with me. And that anger, bitterness, and pain began to slowly devastate and deteriorate the relationships that I had once poured everything into.

I became distant from my husband, retracting from him, not only emotionally, but physically. I was resentful of every attempt he made to encourage me because I couldn't see through the bleakness of my situation.

My daughter, who was a three-year-old baby at the time, just wanted the mommy that cuddled, loved, and doted on her. Instead, what she got was a pseudo-mother who was impatient, angry, and disconnected.

I had drowned out the voice of God completely.

And my relationship with God was, well, non-existent, outside of the one-sided arguments and rants. I kicked and screamed, throwing a constant spiritual tantrum to the point that I had drowned out the voice of God completely.

All because what I expected life to be, wasn't how it turned out, bringing the symbolic umbrella and its pitch-black shadow into every area of my life. The darkness and bitterness took over and began to strangle out the remainder of my white picket fence dream.

It felt like it was taking over...even becoming who I was...

It was bright and sunny outside, but in my umbrella cave, it was dark and dank. I tried to stretch out my legs one by one in hopes of loosening the muscles that were perpetually pulled tight from lack of movement, but they didn't want to cooperate. Even though they were under the water, I could hear my joints creak and crack with the strain, and my bones pounded in unison, rebelling at the forced action. My exasperated body seemed to reflect every emotion that I felt. It was like my body had *become* the bitterness, the rage, and the resentment.

When did I become this way?

I knew that it hadn't started with this physical pain, but that it was birthed in me long before and, left unattended, it had begun to fester. And then I remembered, as a wave of nausea washed over me like the hot tub water, exactly where it all began, and it seemed like I couldn't stop the memory no matter how hard I tried.

Terrorized

I sat in Crystal's office, the white noise machine going, set on high, because I was so paranoid that he could somehow hear us talking. I shook my knee nervously while I picked at a scab on my hand until I felt her staring at me, at which point I shoved my hand under my leg. I was desperately trying to quit the habit of cutting myself, so I found other ways to feel the physical pain that I craved. I was so emotionally broken and unavailable, virtually unable to feel any amount of healthy emotion, tearing off a scab was a perfect outlet for feeling something at all.

She seemed to notice during our last couple of sessions that I was more on edge than normal, but didn't really say too much about it because she knew that I would withdraw again if she pressed too hard. "So, Marlia, I got a call from a resident director in your living area this morning, and he said that you may want to talk about something that happened last night. Do you feel up to it?"

I kept my eyes glued to the carpet and almost without thought, wrapped my arms around myself and pulled my knees to my chest.

"It's okay; he can't hurt you here. He doesn't even know where you are."

My eyes shot up with a desperate look as I blurted out, "He always knows where I am! Always."

He and I had been together, on and off, for about a year, but it always seemed like no matter how hard I tried to get away, I would be sucked back in every time. Initially, my return was out of pity because he played the "I'm a good Christian boy who is just misunderstood" card and moped around depressed. However, within just a couple of months, staying became less of an option and more of a compulsion because of the absolute fear that he held me captive with. He always made me aware that he knew where I was, who I was with, and what I had been doing as a way to control, threaten, and scare me into submission.

He and I had been together, on and off, for about a year, but it always seemed like no matter how hard I tried to get away, I would be sucked back in...

I had entered into the relationship a mostly confident, sparkly, and happy young woman, but in very little time, his verbal abuse, stalking, physical threats, and general oddities had transformed me into a paranoid and fearful girl. Over the past few months, his behavior had become much more erratic and aggressive towards me, but I was too afraid to tell anyone because of what he might do to me, or them.

I closed my eyes as I tried to shut out the events of the night before, but they were burned into my mind.

Crystal, trying to be nonchalant, broke into my thoughts, "Whatever you're comfortable talking about, whenever you're ready."

I sat for a minute, weighing out the risk of exposure versus what she might be able to do to help me. It seemed futile to tell her, but in a rare moment of clarity, I began to lay out the details of the evening, feeling like I was back in it all over again.

With a shaky voice and sweating hands, I started, "I broke up with him a couple of days ago, in hopes that I might actually be able to get away this time, and he took it surprisingly well. I wasn't really convinced that he was telling me the truth, but he promised that he understood and that he thought it was the best thing too. But last night, I was alone, studying in my apartment, and there was a knock on the door. As I walked across the room, I had a strange feeling that I should put the chain lock on the door before opening it, so I did. I asked who it was, and he said 'It's me,' which I didn't think anything about because I thought we were in an okay place. When I started to open the door, I realized I had forgotten to take the chain off, but before I could close the door to release it, he shoved his foot in and slammed himself against it, trying to get inside."

Stopping as I choked on the words and the vomit creeping into my throat, my heart raced as I remembered how frantic and terrified I felt. "I tried to scream, but nothing would come out as he rammed the door with his shoulder again and again. I think at some point he realized that he wasn't going to be able to get in, so he shoved his head between the door and the jam and started yelling at me. I was still trying to shut the door and had my foot braced against the bottom. His head was so far in though and I had to stand so close to hold the door that I couldn't avoid seeing him. His eyes looked crazed, and his face seemed contorted as he hissed at me, 'If I can't have you, nobody will! I'm going to cut you into 122 pieces and send you home in an envelope to your mom, and then I'm going to kill myself!' I started screaming back at him that he better leave because I was going to call the cops. He suddenly stopped, jerked his head out, and ran down the hall. I'm pretty sure he got scared, so I don't think he'll be back."

There was silence in the room as Crystal looked at me, and for a second I felt fairly stupid. I'm not sure if it was because of how ludicrous the story sounded or because I had gotten into that situation and was now seemingly unable to extricate myself from it. After a few moments, Crystal leaned in and put her elbows on her knees, folded her hands together, and made direct eye contact with me.

His eyes looked crazed, and his face seemed contorted as he hissed at me, "If I can't have you, nobody will! I'm going to cut you into 122 pieces and..."

"Marlia, we need to have a different conversation. I'm not sure if you are able to fully see the serious nature of what is happening, so I need you to sign some release waivers."

My head spinning with confusion, I asked, "Release waivers? For what?"

I hated him more and more for doing this to me, and I hated myself for allowing it to happen.

She took my hands in hers, still maintaining eye contact with me in hopes that I might get a more complete understanding, "I need you to sign release waivers that would allow me to testify on your behalf and open your file in a court proceeding if you are not there."

I balked at her statement, "Not there? Where would I be?" And then it hit me like a punch to the gut. She was asking me to allow her to testify as my advocate if he ever did kill me. As she turned to reach for the paperwork, my mouth hung open in disbelief. She handed me a pen and a clipboard stacked with papers, which I didn't even read. I just scribbled my signature next to the "X" on each sheet of paper as quickly as I possibly could.

I hated him more and more for doing this to me with every flick of the pen. And I hated myself for allowing it to happen. Once I finished, I tossed the clipboard back to her and sat back on the couch, angry and disillusioned.

What happened to me? How did I ever let it get this far? God, how did YOU let it get this bad?

At that moment, bitterness wrapped itself around my soul and choked out what was left of the young woman I had been before.

My shoulders drew up in anguish as I felt the desperate helplessness of that memory. Letting the front of the umbrella dip further into the water, I shoved my face under the hot bubbles and gave out a long, but silent scream.

God, how could you let him take so much from me? Why didn't you stop it all?

God, how could you let him take so much from me? Why didn't you stop it all?

Furious, I knew the devastation of that relationship changed the very DNA of who I was or would even become, resonating throughout every aspect of my life and into the very tissue of my physical body.

Isolated and alone, I sat with the smell of chorine thick from the hot tub water, intensified by the black umbrella trapping it in. The pain in my joints began to release, along with the emotion that I fought so hard to hold inside. I could feel the water trickle down my face as it mingled with the tears streaming from my eyes. As I wept uncontrollably, my thoughts slipped back further to my earliest memories of feeling abandoned.

Where Did Everyone Go?

The water felt like needles as it beat down on my 10-year-old head. I could barely catch my breath as I choked through the sobs and steam the shower created. I struggled to even stand, my knees wobbly, wanting to buckle under the weight of the emotion, my hands braced on the slippery wet tile to keep me upright. Leaning my forehead against the wall, I let my arms hang down as my mind raced.

What am I going to do without him?

The feeling of desperate loneliness was absolutely overwhelming for me.

The youngest of my three brothers, the one that was eight years older than me, had just left to go to college in Colorado, and the feeling of desperate loneliness was absolutely overwhelming for me.

Why would he leave me alone like this?

Though there were several years between us in age, he was most like my "big brother," the one who relentlessly tormented me but also the one who was my playmate, and the one I held on the highest pedestal.

God, why would you take him away?

I truly thought my heart was actually breaking apart as I secretly mourned his absence in the shower that day, and for many months, even years, after.

My child's mind couldn't process it at the time, but this loss was more painful because of what had occurred in the years leading up to it. He wasn't the first to leave me. In fact, he was one of many in a long line of people who had seemed to slip away.

My middle brother, who was 13 years older, was the one most excited about my birth and the one who took me on as his real-life doll. He volunteered to take care of me at night so that my mom could sleep, carried me into church perched on his arm with my dress fluffed out, and taught me to dance in our living room to the Bee Gee's. Yet when I was just four years old, and for reasons beyond what my little girl mind could understand, he moved out and left me.

Why did he have to leave?

My oldest brother, fourteen years my elder, was more like a father than a sibling. He was the one that I knew, if anything ever happened to my parents, would be the one to take care of me. Even though he seemed more adult than kid to me, he was also the one always coming up with some sort of prank, teaching me the fine art of table "gross out." However, as children do, he grew up and married his high school sweetheart when I was eight years old.

Why did he have to leave?

And then there was my dad, who just confused me. From the time I was born, he left me every other day for 24 hours, came home for four days straight, and then left again.

Why is he always gone when something bad happens?

Every time there was a traumatic event in my life, like when the cat bit me, when I split my chin open, or when I nearly broke my ankle, he wasn't there. However, his here-now-gone schedule wasn't his fault. It was simply the result of his job as a firefighter, but I didn't understand that. All I saw was that my dad was leaving and I didn't want him to go, which just made me angry. He wanted so much to hold and love me, but I struggled to let him be that close, to trust him, because of the inconsistency of his presence.

And it wasn't just the most important men in my life that seemed to abandon me. Grandparents, aunts, uncles, and cousins left, either from death or divorce, within just a few short years. In my little girl mind, as I tried to process the absence of each person, the only conclusion that I could come to is that they abandoned me or God took them away.

Remember, "Good girls get good things." My expectation was that if someone really loved me, and if I was a good girl, they wouldn't leave, regardless of the circumstance. That I could control the outcome of not only my life, but everyone else's around me by simply adhering to the values and Biblical teachings that I had been raised on. That everything would be perfect, all lollipops and rainbows, without any pain or confusion if I could just do what I was trained to do and be a good girl.

But I tried being a good girl! Didn't I do what You wanted me to?

I screamed into the water as the bitterness, pain, and despair built to an explosive level. My body tightened up with pure rage as I white-knuckled my black umbrella, gritting my teeth until I thought they would splinter. And then a switch flipped inside of me, and even though the water I sat in bubbled with heat, my blood ran cold.

I was done. Devastated beyond repair. Feeling like everything I had ever been taught, everything that I believed and had built my life upon was a lie. I felt like I had held up my end of the deal, but God had surely failed on His. The faith that I thought had been so strong, just months before, shattered into seemingly irreparable pieces.

I'm not doing this Your way anymore.

Chapter 2

Dying for the White Picket Fence

He pierced my heart
with arrows from his quiver.
I became the laughingstock of all my people;
they mock me in song all day long.
He has filled me with bitter herbs
and given me gall to drink.
He has broken my teeth with gravel;
he has trampled me in the dust.
I have been deprived of peace;
I have forgotten what prosperity is.
So I say, "My splendor is gone and all that
I had hoped from the Lord."
I remember my affliction and my wandering,
the bitterness and the gall.
I well remember them,
and my soul is downcast within me.

-Lamentations 3:13-20

Beep...swoosh...beep...swoosh...beep...swoosh...beep...swoosh...

The air in the room felt cold as the starched sheet skimmed across my legs. Alone, I laid completely still on my back, staring up with glassy eyes at the blurry dots on the ceiling, tubes connecting me to machines that provided the soundtrack of my life.

My head felt swirly and disconnected. The IV pumping in the clear liquids made sure of that. I tried to focus, to pull a complete thought together, but the dots on the ceiling kept pulling me away. It was hard to think straight, but even harder to breathe. As I inhaled the oxygen streaming in through my nose and mouth, I could feel myself panting, struggling to push air through the thick cobwebs in my lungs without coughing. The strong metallic taste of blood made me sick to my stomach. My body was exhausted, and so was my spirit. I didn't even try to reason, argue, or negotiate with God anymore. My hope of the "Good Girl getting good things" seemed like a lost dream.

So this is what it feels like to die...

Beep...swoosh...beep...swoosh...

So this is what it feels like to die...

Through the monotony of noisy silence, I heard strained, but hushed whispers in the hallway, which I assumed were those of my husband and team of doctors. I desperately wanted to know what they were saying, what secrets they were sharing, but it just took too much effort to maintain a functional coherence. Sleeping, or whatever it was that I was doing, was so much easier. At least there I could dream of how my life used to be, before all hell broke loose.

Twelve long months of agonizing pain, loss of ability, loss of *who* I was. Twelve long months of medications, wheelchairs, and doctors' appointments that seemed to go nowhere. Twelve long months of raging at God, losing my faith, and questioning where the Good Girl went wrong. They said that it was a sudden and severe onset case of rheumatoid arthritis, but once I started coughing up blood, my general practitioner decided that maybe there was something more that needed to be addressed.

Oh, really? You think so? What was your first clue, genius?

As I dipped in and out of consciousness, I could feel the warmth of my husband's hand cupping mine as he sat next to me. He was my rock, my safe place, but even in my semi-aware state, I could feel his forehead pressed to the bed next to me and hear his constant prayers as he negotiated with God for my life – for our life. As his body shook with emotion, he begged God to heal me, to bring me back to him and our daughter. Long minutes passed by, his hot tears splashing onto my hand and his grip tightening. I could feel his struggle with seeing the "What Is," the horrible reality before him.

"What Is"

"What Is" is the present, the situation that I am currently standing in. It's not what I would be facing in the future, or even in the next hour, but right here, right now.

As I laid there in the hospital, my "What Is" was not an amazingly sweet moment that I wanted to hold onto forever. And it hadn't been for a long time.

In fact, those sweet moments had become fewer and farther between, and I had tried desperately to avoid the real "What Is" for years because it wasn't fun. In truth, it was really painful to lose so many people in my childhood, to scramble to save my life from a deranged boyfriend, to step into ministry under the guidance of someone I loved and then suffer the loss of my mentor, my friend, *and* my calling. It was excruciating to hear that my daughter would always struggle.

It was really painful to lose so many people, to scramble to save my life, to step into ministry and then suffer the loss of my mentor, my friend, and my calling.

And then the pain of this horrible disease that had ravaged my body...

I had always wanted to run from my "What Is" as quickly as possible, so that I didn't have to deal with it or look it in the face any longer than absolutely necessary. I wanted it to just go away, and never return to my life or memory. My "What Is" was so drastically different than I ever could have imagined that disillusionment had crept in and stolen every other present moment, every other "What Is" thereafter.

I had tried to escape the "What Is" by blaming other people for it. I didn't want to see how I may have had a part in creating it.

And my ultimate scapegoat was God. I blamed Him because He let it happen to me, or didn't hear me, or must be punishing me, or I felt like He wasn't holding up the Good Girl deal I felt we had struck years earlier. I had begged and pleaded for Him to supernaturally fix the "What Is" that was hurting, scaring, and inconveniencing me, and when He didn't move fast enough, in the way I thought He should, I refused to engage a "good father" like that anymore.

Time to Surrender

Beep…swoosh…beep…swoosh…

I opened my eyes to little more than slits. Each short gasp of breath felt like I was trying to lift a crushing 400-pound weight off of my chest. Out of the corner of my eye, I caught a glimpse of the nurse looking at me with sympathetic concern as she adjusted the many hanging bags of solutions that were trying to save me. Had it been hours or days? All sense of time and space seemed to elude me, and really, it didn't matter.

"Josh, I think I'm dying." My voice didn't even sound like me, so breathy and weak in between pants for air.

"No, you're not. Don't say that. You're going to be okay." I could see he was trying to be so strong, to not lose himself in the reality of what was happening before him. Trying not to cry so that I wouldn't really know how scared he was or how dire my condition had truly become.

"I can feel it. It's different." I wasn't cold anymore, and I'm not even sure that I could feel my body as I lay in the bed. It almost felt disconnected.

"It's time. We need to pray, Mar. Let's pray right now that God will heal you."

Did he just say we need to pray? For God to heal me? If I could have laughed, I would have. I'm pretty sure that if God wanted to heal me, He would have done it a long time ago, but He abandoned me. I obviously wasn't a good enough Good Girl, or worth listening to. Why do we need to pray? He doesn't listen to us anyway, he says he does, but I'm fairly certain that's a lie too.

I'm pretty sure that if God wanted to heal me, He would have done it a long time ago, but He abandoned me.

His requests for me to pray with him had started months earlier, but since we had been in the hospital, he had pled with a persistent urgency to the point where it felt as if he wanted to shake me by my shoulders in desperation.

He laid his hands on my body and began. "Dear Jesus, will you *please, please* touch Marlia right now? God we know that you are our Divine Healer, and so we are asking that you will do a miracle right now in her body, that You will do what the doctors can't. Please give us peace. Amen... Mar, your turn."

My turn? For what, exactly? To do what I've already done a million times and beg for relief? For Him to just finish it, or me, already? Here goes hoping for nothing.

Before I could even formulate the words in my head, before I even realized with full clarity what I was saying, they seemed to pour breathlessly out of my mouth between the shallow pants,

"Lord, please forgive me..."

"Lord, please forgive me..."

And then it happened all at once – that "peace that passes all understanding" that the Bible talks about – an overwhelming sense, a breaking, a shift in my spirit that could only be brought on by God Himself. It was as if I spoke those words out of a deep longing, a craving from my innermost self that my logical, hurt mind wouldn't let me acknowledge all of those months before. Even in all of my confusion, disillusionment, and anger, I wanted to be in a right place with my Savior. I *needed* restoration before death.

"Whatever Your will is, I'm okay with it. If You will be more glorified by me dying, then let it happen. But if You will be more glorified by me living, then heal me." As I said the words, hot tears rolled out of my eyes, pouring into my ears and puddling in my neck. I was finally ready to relinquish to the journey that began twelve months earlier, regardless of the outcome. Josh leaned in and kissed my forehead with a gentle brush of his lips as he put the oxygen mask back on my face, and then we sat, holding hands, waiting for the inevitable.

The seconds passed into minutes, the minutes into hours, as my mind flooded with memories of my childhood, my parents, my brothers, my friends. My thoughts fast-forwarded to when Josh and I first met. I was just sure that we were only meant to be friends until that fateful second date when I looked up from a pool cue and heard God tell me directly and distinctly that he was going to be my husband. Then, standing at the church altar just sixteen months later, looking deep into his hazel eyes, we promised to love each other for better or for worse, through sickness and health.

We surely never thought we would actually have to do it though, especially not at 31 years old.

And then there was my baby, my Sweetest Sweetness, Savannah. How would she understand, process, and grieve the loss of her mom at just four years old? How would this affect her growing up, being the kid whose mom isn't there for school trips, teacher meetings, first boyfriends, homecoming dances, and graduation. Not to mention her wedding, or the day she births her own baby. I would miss all of it, all of her.

Will she be bitter at God because it wasn't supposed to turn out that way, or will she have a deeper grasp of how God and life works? Oh, Jesus, protect her heart. Please let her never doubt how much you love her... or how much I love her.

A noise jarred me out of my thoughts and brought me back to the hospital room with Josh. I suddenly realized that I could breathe, and not just little short gasps, but enough to where I didn't feel perpetually dizzy. My body felt connected again, with itself and with the cool sheets underneath it. My eyes seemed to clear a bit, and I was able to focus on the drawing taped to the wall that my sweet baby girl had brought for me. As we waited with expectancy for the inevitable, the miraculous had occurred instead!

I could feel my body begin to respond to medication that hadn't been effective before. My lungs, though still not perfect, felt less like I was breathing in Jello. Still weak, I slowly raised my fingers up to the oxygen mask and fumbled to get it off. Josh, thinking that I was delusional, quickly jumped up and gently pushed my hand away so that he could re-situate it on my face.

When I began to speak, still somewhat breathy, but much stronger than before, I looked into his eyes, with a half-crooked smile, "I think it's going to be okay."

Submitting to "What Is"

The "What Is" was messy and not what I expected or hoped for. I had tried to ignore it, excuse it away, and just pretend that it doesn't exist. But none of that helped. In fact, all that had done was land me in a hospital bed...at death's doorstep.

What else could I do? I had to do the only thing I didn't want to do. I had to acknowledge where I was, say I was sorry, and submit to the "What Is."

Maybe it's because I had nothing left. The anger, the bitterness, the disappointment, it all meant nothing when faced with death. I didn't think it was ever going to get better, and I didn't know if blaming anyone made any sense at that point.

Sure, God hadn't shown up the way I wanted Him too, but I hadn't either. I had tried to be the Good Girl, but it wasn't hard to look back and find those moments where I hadn't been – where I had failed.

Maybe that's what this is...just my punishment for all of those bad choices...for abandoning my calling, for getting into that relationship, or...?

But at that moment in the hospital, none of my reasoning mattered. In the instant that I had begun to pray again, my first impulse was to submit to it.

Little did I know it was just the beginning of me learning to submit to my "What Is."

Back on My Feet – Not So Much!

My legs felt like lead as I dragged them along, completely useless in their purpose. I could feel Josh pressed up behind me, his muscled arms wrapped around my waist, trying to be as gentle as possible as he struggled to get me into our home. Frustrated that I couldn't help him, little tears welled up in my eyes. I tried to choke them back so that my daughter wouldn't see them as she excitedly looked at her momma who was finally going to be home with her again.

My mom, who walked ahead, quickly slid the key in the lock, swung the door open, and then turned, giving a sheepish grin with a soft "Welcome home."

As thrilled as I was to be out of the hospital that had been my residence, and at times prison, for three and a half months, this wasn't quite what I had expected for my big homecoming. I guess I thought that because God decided to do the amazing, the miraculous, and literally bring me back from the brink of death, I just figured that He would have finished the job by now. But instead, the legs that had once been strong enough to take me through a 26.2 mile marathon course were now so atrophied from lack of use that it left me here, clinging to my angel-like husband, praying to heaven above that we wouldn't get tangled up, trip, and fall on our faces.

As we clumsily navigated my awkward body into the house, exhaustion fully set in, and I suddenly craved my soft, familiar bed, which just happened to be on the second floor of our house.

Well, that should be fun.

Just as Josh shuffled me around to face the stairs, my eyes landed on what may have just been one of the prettiest things I had ever seen. My chair elevator. We had it installed along the handrail leading up to the second story when we first moved into the house eight months earlier because it was so excruciating to climb the stairs with the joint pain. Every time I had used, or even looked at it before, I wanted to rip it off its track and throw it through a window because though it was helpful, it also represented my utter and absolute inability.

Now, however, I wanted to apologize to it, to even kiss it, ask it's forgiveness, and make up so it would want to play nice by taking me to the top of the staircase and to my blessed bed.

As Josh helped me into the little chair and got me situated, buckling the seat belt so that I wouldn't fall off, he realized that he had forgotten to stop at the pharmacy for my medications, which I was overdue for. "Babe, I really need to go now and get everything because if we wait too long, the pain meds will wear off."

I thought that because God had decided to do the amazing, the miraculous, and literally bring me back from the brink of death, I just figured that He would have finished the job by now.

Oh, mercy, we really don't want that to happen!

That's what I thought, but what I said was, "Of course, I'll be fine. My mom is here, and it's only a couple of steps to the bedroom." Famous last words.

As Josh walked out, shutting the front door behind him, Savannah excitedly pushed the button on the arm of the chair with her little cherubic fingers to start my ascension. I watched her as she stepped, making sure to keep pace with me, gently holding my hand the whole way. As I looked at her, I could feel my heart break.

Where did my baby go? When did she grow up?

It just seemed so unfair that this had also become her life, that she had been robbed of so much, namely the trusting innocence that Mom and Dad would always be around. Just as I reached the point that I could have lost myself in the emotion of that thought, the chair came to a sudden and jolting halt, and Savannah chirped out in her little bitty girly voice, "We're here!"

I tried to smile up at my mom who was now standing in front of me on the stair, hoping that she wouldn't sense my anxiety that was beginning to build.

She smiled back and gave a quick, "Well, are you ready to give it a go?"

My concern at this point wasn't just for me, but for my mom as well. As I looked at her, I knew she was a strong woman, but the reality also set in that she wasn't a spring chicken anymore. All I could think of was that she could fall down the steps and break a hip.

Then we'd be a in a real pickle.

She stepped onto the landing at the top and helped me swing my left foot up to where she was and then gently placed my right foot on the second stair so that I could brace myself.

This will be a piece of cake. I kept trying to convince myself.

"One, two, three!" I pushed up hard on the armrests of the chair, placing the majority of my balance and weight on my upper foot, thinking that would set me up for an easier transition.

My mom, trying to help brace my arms, and Savannah, cheering me on as if I was in an athletic event, kept encouraging me with "There you go's," "You got it's," and "No problem's" as I finished pulling myself up, wanting to do as much of it on my own as possible.

Feeling quite accomplished and a little cocky, I stepped to bring my right foot up so that I could begin the next leg of the journey to my bed.

Just as I thought I was in the clear, I realized that the tips of my right toes were caught on the edge of the stair and I was headed to the floor in super slow motion. As quick as I thought I was moving to recover my stance, I was in reality not quick enough, and so instead of catching myself, I face-planted nose first into my brown low-pile shag carpet, not even able to get my hands up to absorb some of the impact.

There I lay, at the feet of my four-year-old daughter and 67-year-old mother who both gasped in sheer horror at what had just happened.

There I lay, at the feet of my four-year-old daughter...

Really God?!? If this wasn't so funny, it would be tragic.

And so I did the only thing that I could. I laughed and cried all at the same time. My sweet Savannah got her pillow and placed it under my head, covered me with her baby quilt, and then read me her favorite bedtime story to pass the time until Daddy got home to help her Mommy off of the floor. I watched her as she sat cuddled up next to me, nurturing me the best way she knew how, realizing in that moment that my life, our lives, would probably never be the same again.

I may not understand why, God, but I guess it is what it is.

How Long Can I Do This?

The table was set with flowery cups, and the sweet smell of orange spice tea wafted up as it was steeped in the pretty porcelain pot that had been passed down to me. The Spring sun was warm on my back and face, and the birds serenaded me from their perches in the nearby trees while I quietly took it all in.

As I sat at the rusty, old wrought-iron bistro table in the backyard waiting for my mom and Savannah to join me, I opened to the safe white space of my journal to add to the ongoing process that I had documented there.

Jesus, I'm trying really hard not to focus on the difficulty of it all, but sometimes, it just seems overwhelming. What do You want for me in this? I'm tired of asking for help and watching the people around me work so hard because I can't do anything. I'm tired of using this walker and counting on everyone else to make the food, do the laundry, pick Savannah up from school, and... well, the things a good wife and mommy should be doing.

Little tears trickled down my face as I again waited for an answer that seemed like it would never come.

Pen still in hand, I unconsciously pushed aside the metal walker sitting next to me so that I could gently rub my legs which were still weak and sore from physical therapy. As I tried to mentally focus and will the response I wanted from Him, my pen found its way back to the page and asked the real question that plagued me.

God, how am I supposed to deal with it all?

Little tears trickled down my face as I again waited for an answer that seemed like it would never come. But instead of God, I heard the sing-song voice of my girl as she hollered from the open sliding glass door, "Hey Mommy, is the tea ready yet?"

As I looked up from my heartbreak written on paper, I saw His answer, and she beamed at me with a bright, wide smile. She was joyful and full of life as she practically skipped towards me across the grass, carrying a plate of finger sandwiches and cookies that she had proudly made with her grandma. She was completely living in the right now, thrilled with the tea party that was about to happen. It wasn't that she'd forgotten the reality of her momma still being sick, but for her, the way to deal best was a good cup of tea, a pointed pinky finger, and a tasty cookie with her momma and grandma.

Hmm, thank you, Jesus. I know You will help me deal with this one day at a time. I will try to stay here, in the present with You and Savannah.

I had no idea that the real healing hadn't even begun, and that the next step would be the hardest. My Good Girl wasn't going to give up on her white picket fence dream so easily, striving to maintain the façade of perfection or at least the semblance that she could keep it together no matter the circumstance. But God had special plans for us both.

Chapter 3

Mourning My White Picket Fence

———∞———

For no one is cast off
by the Lord forever.
Though he brings grief,
he will show compassion,
so great is his unfailing love.
For he does not willingly
bring affliction
or grief to anyone.
—Lamentations 3:31-33

———∞———

I sat in the chilly office, wishing I had more clothes on and holding the paper gown together, along with what little dignity I had left.

The walls were covered with posters on various health issues like how to know if you have diabetes, or why it's important to get your mammogram, along with others diagramming the anatomy of different "lady parts." My eyes scanned them all, reading every statistic and fact, trying to distract myself from the monotonous boredom of waiting. However, there was one that really caught my attention, and all I could do was stare. It was a poster of this sweet cherubic newborn, all round and perfect with ten fingers and ten toes, smile shining, and utterly beautiful.

My eyes welled up with tears and my heart ached at the prospect of never having another one of those in my arms, let alone my belly, again.

Stop it, Marlia! You don't even know yet. Pull yourself together!

While the Good Girl was still in the middle of scolding me, a knock on the door startled me out of my thoughts. "Mrs. Cochran, how are you today?"

"I'm great. How are you?"

Wow, I am such a liar because I'm not great, and I really don't care how you're doing.

"So, we received the results from your latest blood work, and everything is looking pretty good..." I could feel the smile start to creep up on the edges of my mouth as my eyes darted to the newborn on the poster. "…except for your hormone levels. They are extremely low, suggesting that you have not only started into menopause, but that you have already completely gone through it. What we'll need to do is…"

"I am sorry. At least you have one child though, right?"

I stopped listening at that point because the ringing in my ears turned into a roar, my throat tightened up, and I could feel my lunch churning in my stomach. I still had enough sense to preserve the pasted-on good girl smile and nod my head in agreement with whatever she was saying, which threw me back to the time I sat in the doctor's office for Savannah with that same stupid smile on my face. It seemed like the Good Girl in me wouldn't allow anything less than composed perfection, even when faced with tragic sorrow.

My mind snapped back to the cold room and the paper table liner sticking to the backs of my legs when I heard the doctor say, "Of course, we were hopeful that the results would be different, but when you take the type of chemotherapy that you were on, and then continue to have to take it for so long, the chances were slim. I am sorry. At least you have one child though, right? Go ahead and get dressed, and I'll meet you out front."

I slowly slipped my shirt on one sleeve at a time, in complete shock as my heart broke.

She's right. At least I do have one child. But...

Just as I reached for my jeans, I remembered a prayer that I had prayed just a couple of months before.

"God, you know that we would love to have more children, to be able to give Savannah the brother or sister that she so desperately wants, but if it's not going to be good for me to try and birth them, if my body won't be able to survive it, then I either need you to take away the ability or the desire."

Well, I guess I have my answer. I sure wish it had been the desire instead.

How am I going to tell Josh that he will never have his little toe-headed son to toss a ball around with?

The summer air was sweltering as I walked to my car, but I was numb to it. The very thing I had dreaded would happen had been confirmed. Even if I ever came to a time where my body was stable enough to care for another child, it was impossible to have one anyway.

How am I going to tell Josh that he will never have his little toe-headed son to toss a ball around with? That the other little girl that we've both dreamed of would never be? How am I going to explain to Savannah that she will never get to put her cheek on my belly and feel her brother or sister roll around? That she will be the only child in our family after she has been so excitedly chattering about how she would be such a good big sister?

Imagining the wet, hot tears that would be cried that night, I found myself at the car, braced against the door, starting to feel light-headed from the quick, anxious breaths. As I slumped into the seat, I leaned my head against the blistering steering wheel for support and gripped the sides of my legs to find my bearings.

What if I hadn't run the marathon and had gotten pregnant instead? What if I had gotten better treatment sooner? What if I hadn't been so rebellious and walked away from my calling to ministry? What if I had just been a good girl?

The "What If's" just kept coming, bombarding me like piercing arrows of accusation, each one honing in on my own sense of guilt and inadequacy.

It's all my fault! Our lives have been ruined in so many ways because of me!

Sweat, mixed with tears, ran down my face as I tried to pull myself back from the brink of bitter regret. I looked in my rearview mirror to wipe the mess of makeup with my sleeve, attempting to regain some semblance of composure so that I could drive home without running off the road. I still couldn't shake the "What If's" that dogged me. They just played over and over in my mind.

As I slipped my key in the ignition and slowly turned the car on, I turned the radio up as loud as my ears could take to try and drown out the vicious attack that was being waged in my head.

God, what if I had just listened to You?

Family Heartbreak

We sat holding each other, trying to comfort what could not be comforted. Josh struggled to put on his brave face, but I could tell his heart broke with a deep longing for what would never be.

Through choking sobs all I could push out over and over again was, "I'm so, so sorry. I'm sorry that I did this to us, to Savannah, to our family."

Surrounding me with his strong arms, he kept trying to reassure me through emotion-soaked whispers, "Marlia, it's not your fault. You didn't choose this. You couldn't control it. I'm just so glad I still have you."

As much as I wanted to believe him, I couldn't.

It IS my fault! If I had just listened and been a good girl, I could give you and Savannah what you both want…what I want.

It IS my fault! If I had just listened and been a good girl, I could give you and Savannah what you both want…what I want.

The guilt and regret was consuming me as the "What If's" came flooding back again.

God, haven't we been through enough? Couldn't You fix this, just this once? Please?

Before even giving Him a chance to confirm the answer I was afraid was inevitable, I sat up with a forced crooked smile, wiped my nose, and looked at Josh square in the eyes. "We are so blessed to have Savannah. She is the most amazing kid, so I can't be that upset, right?"

He tilted his head as confusion crossed his face. "Yes, she is amazing," was all he could reply as he hugged me to him tighter.

Losing Daddy

It was the end of one of the longest weeks of my life. Finally having a chance to sit, I kicked off my heels and looked around at the people who still lingered in conversation and the familiar house that we were all in. It was my dad's firehouse of 33 years, the one that he went to every other 24 hours, the one filled with fire trucks, hoses, and rich brotherhood. It is the place that made him a hero to so many, the only Santa some kids will ever know, and a father to men who were fatherless. And they all cried.

They cried...but I didn't. I felt, nothing.

They cried when his body could no longer fight the cancer that had ravaged him. They cried as we gathered, making plans to honor him the way that a godly man and great firefighter should be honored. They cried as the bagpipes played and his casket, covered with the American flag and his helmet proudly displayed, was escorted down the church aisle by his fire-service brothers. They cried as memories were spoken, pictures were shared, and I gave his last message — his desire for them to truly know Jesus as their Savior. They cried when the hollow and melancholy chorus of *Taps* rang out as we placed him into his last physical place of rest. They all cried.

But I didn't. I felt, nothing.

There was a sense of jealousy rising up in my tight chest because they all felt the sorrow, the loss, the pain that I should have been feeling, and wanted to be feeling, but just wouldn't come. I loved my dad, and even with some of our difficulties in understanding each other over the years, I know he loved me, and I would always be his baby girl.

Why can't I cry like everyone else? Why am I so numb to all of it? It's my dad, for goodness sake!

Allowing my eyes to relax and glass over, I could feel myself slip into a stupor when a hand gripped my shoulder and forced me back. I turned my head and then looked up to see that it was connected to a woman I'd known most of my life. "Marlia, you are so strong, speaking at your own dad's funeral. Now that's a feat. Make sure to take care of your mom because it's going to be a tough road."

I smiled and gave the obligatory "Thank you," as I patted her hand that seemed to be squeezing too tight.

Strong? I'm not strong! I'm just doing what I'm supposed to do, going through the motions. How could anyone possibly deal with, let alone feel, this much grief in one year?

Only six months earlier, I had sat in another room filled with family mourning the loss of my mother-in-law. She truly was an answer to prayer that my own mom had prayed since the day I was born — that God would bring a godly man who would cherish me and then godly in-laws that would accept me as one of their own. And she absolutely did by becoming my "Mom-away-from-Mom." She too had valiantly fought cancer for over a year, but ultimately, the illness took over.

> *I held him, our daughter, family, friends, and anyone else who needed to cry, and I just held all of my emotion in.*

Though her spirit was long gone and celebrating her heavenly homecoming, her body still lay in the bed next to where I sat. My mind swam with all of the memories of our time together, hunting through thrift stores for treasures, playing cards on a Friday night, planning holiday meals, vacations to the river or the desert or wherever their timeshare could take us. Memories of a life that was no longer. Even as I thought about all of these things, my emotions remained absent. My mind had begun my standard "shut down and shove it down" until my eyes swept up and met Josh's.

I had been able to hold it together until I saw him. There he was, a grown man with the fortitude of an oak tree, becoming a brokenhearted little boy who desperately wanted his momma back. The pain and sorrow that he felt emanated from his every pore, and because I loved him so very much, his pain became mine. I hurt in ways I had never hurt before, not because of my own sorrow, but because I saw how devastated the love of my life was. He had always been so strong for me, and now, it was my turn to be strong for him.

Stand up and be strong so that he doesn't have to. Now be a good girl and hold it all together.

And so I did. I held him, our daughter, family, friends, and anyone else who needed to cry, to mourn, and I just held all of my emotion in.

"Well, we'd like to open up the floor and hear some of your favorite memories of our Dad." My brother's voice over the microphone brought me back to the firehouse.

"I can remember this one time…" he started in with one of his fondest, and all I could think was how unfazed I was by all of it.

How could I be so cut off from my emotion that I not only couldn't cry at his funeral, but I preached a sermon with no tears while everyone else wept at the loss. What's wrong with me???

Acknowledging and Feeling Loss

I always thought that mourning was an unnecessary waste of emotion. Being the youngest with three older brothers helped to form this thinking. Crying was seen as a sign of weakness and vulnerability, and of course to mourn, a person has to cry. I deduced from that logic that if it is weak to cry or even acknowledge that something hurt me and made me want to cry, then it is best not to feel, to not acknowledge that it bothers me. Hence, the "shut down and shove it down" mindset that I had honed to perfection.

> *How could I be so cut off from my emotion that I could not cry at his funeral? What's wrong with me???*

This was especially true if the loss or hurt wasn't in direct correlation to death or physical pain. If it was just a situation or relationship that hurt, then the pain didn't exist. I was fine and smiled through it, compounding the emotional, spiritual, and mental mess that was already brewing inside of me.

I did this very thing when we sold our business of seven years, the one that Josh and I had built from the ground up together. Though I was angry (read *scared* there) and felt almost as if we were abandoning a child we had birthed, I played it like I was excited because it meant that God had something different, even better, for us. At least that's what I *told* everyone else. Mind you, poor Josh got the brunt of the real way that I felt, but to everyone else, it was the greatest thing that could have ever happened for us.

What I needed to do was to mourn what I felt I was losing. Even though we chose the "What Is" in that situation, I still needed to express my fears of not working with him everyday and losing that closeness that we experienced through it as a family. I needed to allow myself to feel the uncertainty of what my own future held and even acknowledge the "What If's" that would come up. I even needed to give myself the opportunity to have a conversation about how I struggled with the identity that I felt I was letting go of, and how unsure I was that I would find myself outside of it at the other end.

But instead, I bottled it all up and kept moving. I put on the smile and convinced everyone around me that I was fine. I didn't know any other way.

Losing My Freedom

We sat in my nephrologist's office together, nervously waiting for her to come in, passing the time making unrelated small talk. The past couple of years had been fairly uneventful physically because remission was more about just staying on top of my medications and managing the damage that had been done. My heart was back up to a normal function, even after having gone through a dangerous bout of congestive heart failure. My lungs, only slightly diminished from the scar tissue of the grapefruit-sized lesion that had been on the right side, had also healed better than expected as the lesion miraculously shrank to only 3 cm. My sinuses still required daily attention through rinsing to keep them healing, but it wasn't anything that I couldn't handle.

My kidneys on the other hand were a different story all together. While everything else in my body seemed to submit to the healing process, my kidneys refused to go along with the game plan, and so here we sat in Dr. Pappoe's office.

Sitting up on the exam table, my body felt heavy with exhaustion like I hadn't slept in months.

Typically, I went by myself because it was just a check-up and check-in kind of appointment, but the reports given during the previous three appointments were that my kidney function had plummeted.

What if I can't avoid it anymore? I've been able to work around it for five years, but these results…I bet she's not going to let me off the hook this time.

Sitting up on the exam table, my body felt heavy with exhaustion like I hadn't slept in months. I was sleeping though, a lot; and with an average of about 16 hours a day with naps, I should have felt amazing. I had managed to keep Josh from finding out about my new sleeping schedule, but I couldn't hide the fact that I struggled to walk across the living room without becoming breathless.

I happened to look in the mirror that was mounted over the office sink and even with makeup on, I still had a pale, yellow, ashen color to my face that no amount of foundation, concealer, or blush could cover up.

Whew, Girl, you need a tan!

Just as I began to trace the dark circles around my eyes, Dr. Pappoe came in with my big, fat file in her hand, and I quickly perked up with a smile and tried to make my eyes sparkle in hopes that I could fool her. I exerted this energy for nothing, because she knew me too well for that. She had been a constant in this up and down journey from my first hospital stay. She had been with me since the other doctors announced to Josh that he needed to prepare for me to die in that hospital, but she never gave up. She was part of the team that finally struck the proverbial gold with my correct diagnosis of Wegener's Granulomatosis. She, along with my Rheumatologist, Dr. Tremazi, took on the tedious task of explaining that it was a very rare autoimmune disease that affects only about 30,000 people in the entire world and usually 85%-95% of them die before they can be diagnosed, let alone treated.

She was there when I started my treatment of eight rounds of plasmapheresis to spin out the bad plasma where the disease resides and transplant in donor plasma. She was there when I had to take massive doses of prednisone that caused me to gain 60 pounds of water weight in just a couple of weeks. She was there as I started the oral chemotherapy that caused my hair to fall out and felt like Molotov cocktails going off in my belly.

I quickly perked up with a smile and tried to make my eyes sparkle in hopes that I could fool her.

⸻

"You're supposed to be on my side! Quit trying to rat me out!"

⸻

She was there by my bedside, with my family, and she was there now looking me up and down, trying to hide her concern. "So, how are you feeling, Marlia?"

I tried to avoid making eye contact by fixing the crease in my pants and lying through my teeth. "I feel good. Yeah, pretty good."

"Really? Your creatinine level has jumped to over seven, and I'm concerned. I'm thinking that we shouldn't wait any longer."

My voice rose to near soprano as I chirped, "Yeah, but you said that if I felt okay, we would let it go a little longer."

"You're right, I did, but I'm just concerned that if we let it go much further, it could be harder on your body when we finally do start."

Josh piped in, realizing what I was trying to do, "Yep, she's lying." I shot him a look that would have melted him if I'd had laser beams for eyes.

"You're supposed to be on my side! Quit trying to rat me out!"

"Babe, I am on your side. That's why you need to tell her how you really feel."

I looked back to the floor, feeling that little Good Girl in me resurface and wait for the scolding. Sensing my hesitation, Josh spoke up, "She's out of breath. She can't walk the stairs in our house without stopping halfway up. And she seems to be more tired than normal."

Dr. Pappoe looked from Josh and to me, "Are you struggling to breathe?"

I looked up sheepishly and met her gaze, "Maybe a little."

And there it is, dropped like a sonic boom – the 'D' word.

She didn't skip a beat, "And how about your energy level? Do you feel more tired than normal?"

Okay Mar, it's time to come clean. It's all in God's hands and in His timing.

I sighed as I stopped trying to hold myself up and just let my shoulders slump. "I don't have any energy. I'm exhausted all the time."

"How much are you sleeping?"

"About 16 hours a day."

Now Josh was the one with laser beams for eyes as he balked at my answer. "I'm sorry, did you just say 16 hours a day? Why haven't you told me?" He looked at Dr. Pappoe and continued, "I didn't know that she was sleeping that much, or I would have made sure she was in here sooner." Then he looked back at me, "Seriously, Mar, why are you messing around? We've come too far to let this happen. I know you don't want to start dialysis, but I need you here."

And there it is, dropped like a sonic boom — the 'D' word.

Dr. Pappoe, seeing the gravity of the situation, jumped in, "Marlia, I know that I told you I would let you go a little longer, but I really think it's time. I think your body has reached its limit, and it's time for us to step in and get you going on dialysis. I'm sorry. I know that you're disappointed. I'll step out for a minute and let you guys talk it over."

Sigh. I'm just too tired to argue anymore.

As the door closed, I could tell Josh was upset that I hadn't been truthful, and I waited for the lecture. But it never came. Instead, he gently took my hand, "Mar, I know you were hoping that it would never come to this, but our goal has always been to keep you as healthy as possible as long as possible, and the only way that's going to happen is with dialysis. Think of Savannah and me, if for no other reason."

Big tears that had been welling up in my eyes while he spoke now splashed over and down my cheeks. "I know. I'm ready now." I agreed, but what I really wanted to do was run out of the room, out of the office, out of my life.

Sigh. I'm just too tired to argue anymore.

With that, he opened the door and called for Dr. Pappoe to return to the room before I could change my mind. She also wasn't wasting any time because she came in with paperwork ready for my admittance to the hospital so that they could start the process the next day. "Marlia, I know it's not what you wanted, but I think you will be much happier once you start. You will feel so much better."

Resigned to the idea that I couldn't talk my way out of it, I chuckled, "Yeah, it's definitely not what I was hoping for, but God has a purpose for this too. I serve a mighty God, right?"

I had absolutely experienced the truth of that statement multiple times in my journey, and yet it was completely the good girl thing to say. In all honesty, my heart broke because I knew my life, our life, was about to flip upside-down…again. More than anything, I was devastated that God was allowing us to take one more step further away from our "normal," and how things used to be.

Mourning "What Was"

I stood at the sink doing dishes when Josh bent down and kissed me on the cheek.

Hmph, the cheek? What about the lips? I sure miss kissing his lips.

Sensing my frustration as he got ready to walk out the front door, he shot back over his shoulder, "It's not worth the risk of you getting sick."

Yeah, yeah.

A bit winded from washing, I finished up the last pot and looked out the window that peered over our backyard. Savannah was

I had been a super active mom, a super equal partner, a super accomplished member of the ministry and business community... Superwoman.

climbing on her jungle gym and running back and forth with abandon. Suddenly, she finally looked up and caught me watching her and waved her hands for me to join her in play.

I smiled back at her with a sense of sadness because I knew I wouldn't be able to keep up, already too tired from washing the dishes.

Oh, baby, I sure wish that I could.

As I plopped myself into the kitchen chair, a yearning for how our lives used to be grew into a deep sadness, and then fear, that it would never be the same.

God, it's been so many years, and I just want our normal back. It was so much better then, and I can't see how it could ever be that good again.

There's a Cape in My Closet…Or at Least There Used to Be

Realizing that our lives would never be the same again, I struggled with the loss of normalcy, life as it was before I became sick. I went from being able to go anywhere at anytime with energy for days to constantly worrying about how my body would respond at any given moment and how that would put me back in the hospital. I had been a super active mom, a super equal partner, a super accomplished member of the ministry and business community…

Superwoman. I felt like I had lost my ability, a lot of who I was, and what I used to define me.

It was so good to feel like I was in control of my day and how I felt. I could go, and do, and be without hesitation. I could run with my daughter, kiss my husband, network a room for hours. Life was good. Will it never be normal again?

As I sat there at the kitchen table, remembering moments from the few years before I was sick, I was suddenly struck by reality.

I guess I wasn't really happy the way I imagined I was. I mean, I love Josh and Savannah and wouldn't trade them for the world, but I wasn't happy. I'm not sure what it was, but something was missing.

I pulled myself up and watched Savannah through the window again.

Maybe it's because I walked so far away from my calling. It didn't matter what superhero wife, mom, or community member thing I did, something always felt like it was missing.

Tired of Being Numb

It had been three months since my dad had passed away, and I sat for the first time since then with my journal open, finally ready to converse with God again. As I put pen to paper, the dam broke, and I couldn't keep up with the flowing thoughts.

"I'm not even sure what to say, let alone feel. I have been numb since my dad passed away. Unable to feel, cry, write. I don't think I'm angry, just so tired. I have the sense of being caught in the ocean with wave after wave crashing on my head, unable to get out from under it or to catch my breath. I need relief and to rest in You, but I've felt like I have just been sitting in silent darkness. I realized last week that part of my struggle is that I've felt the need to put on the strong, brave, joyful face for everyone. How can I write a book about joy and not be able to find/choose joy even in the midst of so much death? I know logically that's an unrealistic expectation, but I think the Good Girl in me thought it was required. It wasn't authentic. I feel stuck — like I'm not going to be able to move forward until I really feel the loss of my dad, mom-in-law, and my own health. God, show me how to feel and mourn. I haven't done it, I don't think, since I was a kid. Show me how to find joy in the midst of it. Make the next step plain."

He wasted no time…

Chapter Four

Wait...What About the Fence?

I called on your name, Lord,
from the depths of the pit.
You heard my plea: "Do not close
your ears to my cry for relief."
You came near when I called you,
and you said, "Do not fear."
You, Lord, took up my case;
you redeemed my life.
Lord, you have seen
the wrong done to me.
Uphold my cause!

-Lamentations 3:55-59

We sat in a tight circle, a little dazed because of the earliness of the morning. Two of the ladies sat cross-legged on the floor, and the rest of us snuggled down on beanbags. "So, how's everyone doing?" Amanda smiled at the group.

On the drive out that morning, I had been wrestling with my own set of "What Ifs." "What if God punished me with this disease?" "What if I hadn't left the ministry?" "What if I hadn't been so stubborn?" And the one that always caused the greatest angst was the "What if I had just listened to God in the first place?" Even as I sat and listened to the other women sharing, I struggled to stay present to what was being said because the "What Ifs" played over and over in my mind.

When the circle had wound its way around and it was my turn to give my weekly update, all I could do was tell them the story that started all the "What Ifs" in the first place.

"It was about six months before I became ill, and I was standing in my office, frantically pulling papers together for a meeting that I was already late for. I don't even remember what the meeting was for or who it was with, but at the time, it seemed to be the most important meeting of my life. I prided myself on being able to keep dozens of plates spinning without dropping, but I had a sense that they were teetering on an unknown edge that could destroy me.

"I was a PTA mom, house church leader, growing two businesses, training for a marathon, and essentially running from God. He and I had a bit of a falling out after Savannah was diagnosed, and I couldn't grasp why He would do that to her, to us, to me. I thought

I had fixed most of it, but there was still a deep-seated and bitter wounded-ness that kept Him at arms length, and kept me on the move.

> *"Do you hear me?" I looked to see who was in the room, knowing full well that no physical person was there.*

"Just as I shoved the last stack of papers into my leather attaché case, pushed my hair out of my eyes, and grabbed for my car keys, there came a soft but firm, 'Do you hear Me?'

"My heart raced as I spun around, dropping my purse and everything in it. I looked to see who was in the room, knowing full well that no *physical* person was there. As I stooped down to quickly stuff everything back into my purse, feeling angrier that I was now running even later. He said it even louder, 'Do you hear Me?'

"Still trying to ignore that I even heard anything, I gathered up my things with shaky hands and set them on the desk to rearrange them before bolting out the door. Again, but with a gentler and almost pleading tone, He questioned, 'Do you *hear* Me?'

"Irritated, I shot back, 'Yeah, I hear You,' and then snatched up all that had distracted me, leaving the room and God behind."

I looked up at the women in the circle, thankful that all eyes were full of love, not judgment. Taking a deep breath through the tears, I felt ready to continue.

"Okay, so fast-forward to six months later, I get sick and one of the things that goes through my mind again and again as I sit in the hot tub is that if I had just listened to Him, if I had just been obedient, if I had just been a good girl, He wouldn't have had to punish me like this. That when He asked if I heard Him, He was telling me I'd better listen up, or else, and I ignored Him instead. I knew He was calling me to focus, slow down, and ultimately come back to my calling, but I wasn't ready to let go of how I felt He had failed me. And so, He broke me. He made me sick so that I would have to listen. It's all my fault! The pain, the fear, the trauma for Josh, Savannah, and my family…the financial devastation, no more babies…all of it is my fault! What if I had just listened?"

"What if He wasn't trying to 'break you' at all?"

The ladies sat quiet for a moment, the room heavy with emotion, allowing my words to settle in. I could feel my muscles tighten as I struggled not to run out of the room. The "ugly cry" was just waiting to come out. When it had come to the point of almost feeling awkward with silence, Pastor Tami finally spoke up, "I know you think that this has all been a punishment, but what if it wasn't a warning that He would 'break you' at all, but a loving warning meant to save you?"

The hair on my neck and arms stood up, "Huh? What are you saying?"

Her voice soft, she said it again, "What if He was warning you to save you, not to punish you? What if he was trying to tell you that something bad was happening in your body, and if you didn't slow down, then you would become sick? Isn't that who He is, our salvation? Isn't that what He did as our Father — sent His Son to die for us so that we could experience His saving grace and unconditional love? Couldn't He have been making you aware of what was going to happen or what could be coming, trying to prepare you for it, or even prevent it?"

> *Is it possible that I have two degrees in theology, and yet had my picture of God and me all wrong this whole time?*

I was stunned, and if I could have fallen down, I would have. It felt like an atomic bomb of restorative understanding had just exploded in my brain and in my heart! I was outwardly speechless at the thought of what she had just verbalized, but internally, a barrage of questions flowed one right after the other.

Could that actually be true? Could He have been warning me to save me? Could it be that all of this isn't a punishment, but just What Is? Could He actually be the Good Father He claims to be? Is it possible that I have two degrees in theology, and yet had my picture of God and me all wrong this whole time?

I Get It Now

It seemed like I couldn't park the car fast enough. I grabbed my backpack out of the passenger seat, slammed the car door, and ran into the house. Josh, already home and reading with Savannah on the couch, looked up to see me skid through the front door as I tossed my bag to the floor. "You've got to hear what happened today in my breakthrough session with the ladies!"

Savannah, sensing that this conversation was one that would be less exciting for her than a kids' show, jumped up, kissed my cheek, and scooted into the den. Before I could even sit down next to Josh, the tears had already started pouring out of my eyes and down my cheeks.

Suddenly, I saw God for what He had been all along…

My husband, knowing that I'm not one to easily cry, leaned over to hug me, "Babe, what's wrong? Are you okay?"

Struggling to get the words out, I choked back a sob caught in my throat as I began to answer. "I get it now. The thing that I have missed this whole time! I have been so wrong and just couldn't see it, but it changes everything! God was warning, not punishing me! He was just trying to save me!" And then I couldn't talk anymore because as I wept deep sobs of realization that came from the deepest part of my spirit, my heart was being healed.

I had lived the past six years feeling condemned and abandoned, missing one of the best parts of my Abba Father — His real and true love for me. Suddenly, I saw God for what He had been all along, but my bitterness had kept me from accepting — a Daddy trying to protect His girl…and not because I was a good girl, but just because I am HIS girl!

Over the next hour, Josh sat with me as I poured out everything that Pastor Tami and Amanda had helped me to see — what my Heavenly Father had been trying to show me for so very long.

The God-Matrix: Redefined

Still trying to figure out how all of the pieces fit together, I pained over the concept of God truly being a good Father who gives good gifts. For so long, I had seen Him as having given me this awful disease, failing me by allowing Savannah to be born with microcephaly, and forgetting about me when I felt that so many people were "abandoning" me as a child. There was still a question that I just couldn't shake and would always rise up in my mind, heart, and even out of my mouth: *If He truly is a good Father, then He wouldn't let these things happen. Good Fathers protect their children, and don't allow pain and suffering, right?*

And then it hit me! I snapped my head up and blurted out, "It's like The Matrix!"

I decided to say it out loud one morning in another breakthrough session with my coach and fellow authors.

"Okay, so I'm seeing my body healed, and I can see the spiritual growth happening. We're even getting into a groove with our new normal, but I still can't quite reconcile the disparity that I feel between who God says He is throughout scripture and who I feel like I have experienced Him to be. I'm being a hypocrite because I'm speaking to groups of women about their disillusionment with their What Is, and I'm hiding the fact that I'm still stuck in some disillusionment of my own and the God that I feel created it."

Pastor Tami, sensing my spiritual and emotional angst as I held my head in my hands, asked, "What do you *know* to be true?"

What do I know to be true? What do I know to be true?

And then it hit me! I snapped my head up and blurted out, "It's like *The Matrix*!" They all looked at me with blank stares, not quite making the connection.

"In the movie, *The Matrix*, there is Reality and then there is the Matrix. The Matrix is a made-up cyber dream world based in assumptions, expectations, and ideas that create the pseudo physical world. But the Matrix is all a lie. The people who continue to live in it view their past, present, and future through these lies, and thereby cannot see it for what it really is or what it could be. Reality, on the other hand, is the truth. The only way to leave the Matrix and get to Reality is by choosing to take the red pill which begins a process of stripping away the dream world's blinders of all false expectations, damaging assumptions, and unfounded ideas that the person had believed before." I could see that they were starting to put it together.

"I have been essentially living in a God-Matrix."

The God-Matrix for me had been years of assuming, consciously and subconsciously, that God was critical, unforgiving, and the great punisher of "bad girls." There was a part of me that believed in the core of His character — He was spiteful and distant — basing His love for me on how perfect I could be or how much of a good girl I was. I walked through life expecting Him to be hugely disappointed in me, and so I was constantly working and striving to be better.

I had over-filled my mind with thoughts and ideas of God, when what I needed was to be finally trans-formed by the grace of living in God.

"Why do we believe this stuff about God?" Amanda interjected. "I mean, it goes against basic parenting instincts, doesn't it? Do you sit around and watch Savannah, to try and catch her doing something wrong? Do you give her love based on how good she is?"

"No, and it's weird, because I knew it in my head, but I just wouldn't let it sink into my heart enough to believe it. He's like us. I mean, we're like Him, in that we love our children so much that we do whatever we can to keep them from getting hurt. If Savannah kept trying to touch a hot stove, I would warn her again and again, because the last thing I want is for her to feel pain, but ultimately, if she wants to touch that stove, she's going to figure out a way to do it. When she finally does, she's going to get burned, and the pain from it isn't a punishment from me, just the natural consequences of her choice, of her not listening to my warning. It's the same with God and us. He warns us, but if we don't listen, the natural consequences can be extremely painful, not because He caused it, but because they become the "What Is" of our choices. I finally get it now!"

I looked around at a room full of smiling faces, and answered my own question: "Just like in the movie, the God-Matrix is a lie, and my only out is to choose to take the red pill of understanding how to live in His Father Heart and see His faithfulness in keeping His promises. He doesn't *want* to discipline me, He only wants to walk closely with me in the intimacy I was created for."

Goodbye, matrix. Hello, Loving Father!

It was as if all of the schooling I had ever had, all of the classes I had ever taken, all of the books I had ever read, all of the lectures that I had ever heard were inconsequential. I had over-filled my mind with thoughts and ideas *of* God, when what I needed was to be finally transformed by the grace of living *in* God. He wanted to share the parts of His heart that mine lacked and make me whole again, to *really* make it all good.

Receiving a Father's Heart Transplant

Days went by and my mind continued to reel with my new understanding.

Oh my gosh!! I have been letting the static noise of past experiences and false expectations drown out the truth of who He really is! I have missed out on so many years of intimacy that He has been longing for. So many opportunities that I could have seen the real Him, and even the real me. What if He wants more for me? What if He is offering me a heart transplant?

When I was shown that my heart was diseased with the lies of who I thought God to be and willingly submitted to the surgeon hand of my Divine Father to cut away the infection, He tenderly began to transplant in the parts of His heart that would heal me. I suddenly felt His desperate desire for me to see Him in full truth so that I could see myself and every "What Is" in light of it. I could feel His longing to push the bitterness out to make room for joy.

Seeing Me Through His Heart

I doodled a bouquet of daisies on the corner of the journal page while trying to gather my thoughts, but then quickly started to write.

I was always afraid that if I wasn't perfect enough, at some point, I would max out God's patience with my imperfection...

"I think I'm still stuck in the 'good girls get good things' thinking. I know You desire me to be close to You and in Your presence, but I have a hard time not thinking that good things are conditional to my time with You, my 'good behavior.' I'm not looking to know what the minimum investment is to get a great return, but I guess it's that I always wonder how human I can be? At what point of imperfection do You pull away?" I paused and took a deep breath, searching for truth. Waiting for His truth.

"But then I read of Your unfailing love for me in scripture. I know in my head that it is absolute truth, but I still struggle with trusting it in my heart. Why is that? The little girl in me reconciles that the reason so many bad things happened when I was young was because I wasn't good enough. And that ultimately, Your love is conditional too."

I used my pen to push up my glasses as I waited for His response.

Quickly, and without hesitation, He gave the definitive answer I needed. "That is a lie. I love you unconditionally, and I will never leave you. You were not a bad girl. Those things happening had nothing to do with you. I allowed you to experience it so that you would have it as part of your story. I do not pull away from you, I just widen the perimeter of who you see Me to be. By widening Myself, you can draw deeper into Me to know and understand a greater part of who I am…and my unconditional love for you. "

Granted, I knew it in my head, having been told this since I was a little girl, but this truth was finally beginning to make its way into a deeper place.

"So, You don't just unconditionally love me *in spite* of who I am, but *because* of who I am?"

"Yes," was all He said.

I was always afraid that if I wasn't perfect enough, at some point, I would max out God's patience with my imperfection, and He would be done with me. I looked out the nearby window as my thoughts trailed off the page.

What if my being perfect or imperfect has nothing to do with how much He loves me? What if it's not a qualifier for His affections? What if He simply asks for an authentic me who is perfectly imperfect as I seek out more of Him in my daily journey?

———⟨✧⟩———

My body wracked with sobs, my ribs ached, my eyes burned… I wept so hard that I almost lost myself in it until I heard God whisper into my spirit.

———⟨✧⟩———

"Marlia, maybe it's time for you to remove the 'What ifs'…"

"What?"

"You are My absolute favorite. Yep, I adore you and think about you morning, noon, and night. I smile when I see you, which is all the time because I can't take My eyes off of you, and I can't wait to talk to you. You are My princess, and I crave for you to be a Daddy's girl who sits in My lap, looking at Me longingly, telling Me all of your hopes, dreams, and sorrows. I lavish you with kisses throughout the day, whispering sweet love songs in your ear. I pour out My unending affection because you are Mine. I want you to feel how good it is to be the favorite daughter of the Most High King!"

It was the best love note ever written, and I could almost feel the truths that He was pouring into me finally sinking from my head into my heart.

As quickly as the love had washed over me, the questions followed. Flicking the pen back and forth in my hand, I thought for a minute and then asked, "The situations, the people, the 'What Was,' the

'What Is,' that causes me sorrow, sadness, and tears, what about that?"

He was quiet for a second, allowing the weight of the question to settle on the page. "It grieves Me too. I feel everything you feel. I'm your Dad and what breaks your heart, breaks Mine. I want for you to bring it all to Me so that I can comfort you too."

This truth was a hard one to swallow because I had pushed Him so far away at varying points in my journey that I couldn't fathom how He would even care at all. I felt like He had been so distant, and there was a part of me that was still utterly convinced that I had brought this all on myself. I couldn't imagine that He would empathize on any level. Again, I had always been taught that He stays close to the brokenhearted, but I was unable to grasp the depth of this.

"I absolutely want the very best things for you. If you'll let Me, I will unfold a greater plan for your life than you could ever imagine."

Then, unexpectedly, I started to cry. One tear, then the next, came trickling out of my eyes, falling onto the journal page. And they kept coming, harder and faster, until I wasn't just crying anymore but weeping. My body wracked with sobs, my ribs ached, my eyes burned, and my throat became sore. I wept so hard that I almost lost myself in it until I heard God whisper into my spirit, "Now you have a sense of the sorrow I felt for you, with you, the whole time."

Overwhelmed with His love, I bowed my head, closed my eyes, and allowed all of the pain, anger, and fear I had been feeling for the last two decades of my life to begin to release as the memories flashed through my mind.

What if He was never distant, but in the muck and mire of it all right along with me? What if in the moments that I cursed Him for not caring or loving me enough to take it all away, His heart was shattering along with mine because He saw my pain…felt my pain? Just like my heart breaks when I watch Savannah feeling hurt and angry with me…and not letting me comfort her.

As I tried to pull myself together and catch my breath between little crying chokes, He spoke another truth that made it difficult for me to exhale. "I absolutely want the very best things for you. If you'll let Me, I will unfold a greater plan for your life than you could ever imagine."

I shifted in my cozy chair, trying to let this one sink in over the doubts I'd held onto for the last six years.

If someone would have tried to tell me this truth about God at the beginning of my journey six years ago, I would have laughed and said they were delusional. I couldn't see how a God who wants the best things for me would have ever let something so devastating to my body, mind, and spirit happen.

To think that His plan — my illness playing some part in it because He already knew what would happen — could possibly be greater than anything that I could dream up, just seemed ludicrous. I was so stuck in the assumption that my "What Is" was a punishment

— and that it was all a consequence of God's disappointment dealt without any grace or mercy — that I couldn't see what was actually happening.

What if all of my experiences, all of my pain, all of my disillusionment are what brought me to this moment? To experiencing the unconditional love of my Father?

And, maybe more importantly, I wouldn't have come to a deeper *real* understanding and dependence on God, but instead would have continued trying to keep the plates spinning as I ran through life.

I would have lost out on this moment of experiencing Your Father heart. I would have missed the chance to see how You keep Your promises and that, truly, Your best is yet to come, and it is so good. Hallelujah!

In the Restoration

A few weeks later, at my parent's cabin, I stole away for just a few minutes and sat on the second story deck looking out over the valley of pine trees that I had watched grow over the past 27 years. Everything coming up from the ground was so green and the sky so blue that it almost seemed to be enhanced in technicolor. I tried to capture this moment and then closed my eyes to absorb it through every sense. I drew in a deep breath, filling my nose and lungs with the earthy scent of high altitude mountain air tinged with the savory richness of grilling meat that made my mouth water with anticipation. It was the end of summer, and though it was warm during the day, as the sun began to drop, the breeze became cool against my face.

As a sense of self-pity began to creep in along with the little tear at the corner of my eye, God whispered just slightly above the breeze...

Around the back of the cabin, the sweet sound of Savannah giggling rang out as she played hide-n-seek in the nearby woods with her two older cousins. My mom's voice soon mingled in melodically as she quietly sang "The Old Rugged Cross" while washing dishes on the other side of the kitchen window. I even picked up the faint sound of crunching ice as Josh and my brother Don-Alan took turns churning the crank on the homemade ice-cream maker, which would be the crown jewel of the meal.

Almost without realizing it, I ran my hands out on either side of my legs along the glossy, buttery smooth wood of the bench marked in memory of my dad and smiled at the thought of how much he loved this place.

So many memories over so many years.

Long summers of playing at the lake, ice cream at the snack shack, cruising up and down the hill on the 4-wheeler, and sleeping on the deck beneath the stars. Cold winter weekends full of snowmobiling through the back woods, inner-tubing down the snow run, drinking hot cocoa by the fire, and playing card games that ran late into the night. I cherished each one while they played through my thoughts like old movie reels, and I felt a deep sense of gratitude.

I am so blessed to have had the opportunity to make such amazing memories. I wonder if I will ever have the chance to make more to add to my collection?

As a sense of self-pity began to creep in along with the little tear at the corner of my eye, God whispered just slightly above the breeze, "Look around. Listen well. You already are."

The normalcy of my life pre-illness that I had grieved so deeply was never going to be the same again, but I realized in that moment, with that quiet reminder, that God was giving me something that He assured would be even better than I could ever imagine — a new normal. And not just a "normal" of regular proportions, but one that was filled with a hope and a future.

All that I felt I had lost or had been stolen away would be fully redeemed, fully restored, and He promised it to be good.

So much of it already is good. My health is improving, my family is happy and healthy, and my relationship with my good Father is back on track. And He promises it will just keep getting better.

I leaned back on the bench, crossing my arms behind my head and looked up as the clouds lazily floated by. I took in a deep breath and smiled.

I can't wait!

Could It Have Been Different?

I sat in my office, looking out the sliding glass door that was positioned directly across from me. The sun was bright, and the heat radiated into the room, making it almost too warm. My Bible was laid out in front of me on the desk, along with my devotional and my journal. With pen in hand, I was ready to write.

I had been looking through scripture for weeks, and I knew there had to be an explanation for all of it, I just couldn't figure out what it was. God had been clear through the conversation I had with Pastor Tami and Amanda that my "What Is" surrounding my illness wasn't a punishment. And yet, as reassuring as that was, it opened up a Pandora's Box of questions. I still wondered if I had just listened, slowed down, gone back to my true purpose at that point, if it would have all turned out differently.

Continuing to sit, I tried not to be distracted by the fact that I had an inbox full of emails that needed answering, a pile of laundry that needed washing, and chicken that needed to be pulled from the freezer. Trying to slow down had always been difficult for me, and I knew that the hyper-speed of my life was part of what got me sick.

To practice slowing down, I had recently started trying to use a new way of communicating with God. Well, new to me at least. I would ask a question and then sit and listen, waiting for His response, in hopes that I might actually get answers. I know, novel idea since we're encouraged throughout scripture to be still and listen for His voice, however there was a little part of me that was working through the whole "I wonder if He's actually going to show up for me" way of thinking.

While I waited, I decided to journal a bit about some of what was running through my mind and again posed the question that weighed heaviest on my heart: "How would it have been different if I had just listened?"

I heard God speak into my spirit, "It wouldn't have been different."

A little stunned, I quickly wrote it down before I asked my next question: "So would it still be the same?"

His response came back quicker this time, "Yes, but no. It would have been the same physical situation but a different spiritual response. Listening would have prepared you spiritually for what was coming. "

To practice slowing down, I had recently started trying to use a new way of communicating with God.

Almost forgetting to write down what I heard Him telling me, I asked, "Could I have changed it?"

And then God posed a question right back to me, "Would you want to?"

Now, it was my turn to answer the questions, "Yes, but no. If I could have the message without the pain, but I know that I couldn't."

His next response floored me with the realization of the gravity of it. "Neither could Jesus. He chose the pain for the message."

My hand hurt from writing so fast, and I was a bit dumbfounded that we were having this crazy back and forth conversation. He was quiet for a bit, I think giving me a rest and a minute to let it sink in. He then continued, "Take up your cross and follow me."

Oh mercy.

A few minutes later, after my breathing had slowed, I continued with my questions. "But how does this all fit into the book?"

"They need to really see me as good and as their salvation. Not their current view of me as the One who just watches and waits for them to screw up so that I can jump on them. Sound familiar?"

So familiar, so painfully familiar.

What if without the journey that I have walked, I would never have the testimony that I have?

Suddenly, I felt a burning in my chest, a sense of anticipation, even excitement, as I began to see that I wouldn't have a story that God could use to speak to other women that would offer them healing if all of this hadn't happened.

I'm not sure I would have changed it.

Seeing Others through His Eyes

One of the moms that I had just finished speaking to slowly approached me, and I could tell that she had been crying a bit. "Marlia, your story really moved me."

"Thank you. Disillusionment and trying to be the good girl is hard, isn't it?"

What if without the journey that I have walked, I would never have the testimony that I have?

"Yes, it is, but actually, what really got me was when you mentioned that you had been in that rough relationship and didn't quite know how to handle it because of your good girl upbringing."

"Oh, okay. Well thanks." I smiled, but was a little thrown off because it's not at all what I was expecting her to comment on.

She continued, "I'm the head of a ministry here at the church that is hosting a conference about human trafficking and slavery. I think your story would be great during the panel discussion. Would you be willing to come?"

Slightly confused, I responded, "Um, I'm absolutely willing to help, but I'm not really sure how my story applies."

"You may not have been trafficked or enslaved, but you were exploited by that guy and didn't see it coming or how to get out of it. I think it would be really powerful for the parents to hear your story so they can prepare their kids for something like that…and the kids to hear so they will know what to look out for."

Trying to keep my voice from shaking, "Wow, I have never really thought about it like that before. Sure, I'll be there. Just send me the details."

I walked away, feeling a little queasy at what I had just committed to. I had spoken many times on my journey, on the disillusionment, on the faith struggle that I experienced, but I had *never* spoken openly about the details of the abusive relationship that I was in before meeting Josh.

Exploited? Hmm, that's an interesting twist.

As I drove home, I thought about the gravity of that word and all that it implied. Suddenly, I felt the rage that I had pushed down a long time ago overwhelm my system.

My insides churned with hatred as I gripped the steering wheel tighter and tighter, trying to keep the car centered in the lane. I despised the fact that thinking about him and what happened could still trigger this kind of response, so many years later.

Crying and exasperated, I practically shouted at God, "When am I going to be done with this?!?"

I could feel the presence of the Holy Spirit in my car as He came to comfort me. The Fatherly voice of God answered, "When you can forgive him."

I balked at the words and practically gagged as I said them out loud to myself, "Forgive him? How is that even possible? He was a monster — the devil incarnate! He claimed to know You, but he just used that to manipulate my innocence!"

"Marlia, your hatred and unforgiveness does nothing to him, but it eats you up. It robs you of the joy and peace that I have for you."

Fuming and hurt that God was asking me to do the seemingly unreasonable, I shot back, "So I'm just supposed to let it all go? Let him off the hook? Like it was all okay?"

"By no means am I excusing or saying that what he did to you was okay. I am still your Righteous Father who promises justice for His children, who hates what was done against you. But understand, it is Mine to take care of, not yours to hold on to."

Crying and exasperated, I practically shouted at God, "When am I going to be done with this?!?"

He paused, as if to allow what He was saying to sink deep into my heart. It had been so many years, and I was so weary and worn from being bound by this consuming hatred. "So, what does this mean? How can I possibly forgive him?"

"What if his perception of love was so greatly distorted, because of never experiencing it in a healthy, Godly way that it made him broken, scared, and hurt too? What if he was so deeply damaged by something that happened to him, that it shattered his ability to fully understand how to love someone as I desire for them to be loved?"

Starting to see it in a small way, I still struggled to fully grasp it.

"Marlia, he was human, fallen, with a sin nature that he allowed to overtake him...but he is still in need of My saving grace to be whole. I need you to see him how I see him. He is still my son that I love and desire — a lost child my heart breaks for. Can you understand that? What if you could see him how I see him? Are you willing to look at him through My eyes?"

I pulled into my driveway, overcome with emotion, finally beginning to experience the deeper heart understanding that God wanted to use to heal me.

"Abba, please help me to see him, and whoever else I need to forgive, through your Father heart."

But before I could do that, I had to see myself through His Father heart...

The Good Girl-Matrix

"Do you realize this God-Matrix idea really changes everything? Not only how I see God, but how I see myself, my purpose, and my relationships too?"

Feeling where I was going with this, Amanda smiled and allowed me to work it out, "How so?"

"It is impossible for me not to be changed because I am a direct reflection of Him, having been made in His image. If good girls get good things, and a lot of what I 'got' didn't seem good, then I must have been bad because I wasn't trying hard enough; hence I expected nothing less than perfection from myself, which was always unattainably disappointing. Wow! That is such a lie!"

The "aha" happening felt huge, and I took a deep breath before continuing, "The Good Girl was a façade that I maintained to protect myself from vulnerability, judgment, and condemnation. I felt like the Good Girl persona allowed my parents to be proud of me, garnered respect from my peers and trust from those that I ministered to. But *she* also forced a double life of inauthenticity, lacking any real transparency, because my value was based in what I did, and who I pretended to be, rather than who I really was as a Princess of the Most High King. *She* kept me in shame and guilt, not allowing me to truly confess, repent, and be forgiven openly for what I struggled with. I couldn't fully use my experiences and mistakes as lessons for myself and others that God could redeem because *she* had an impeccable image to uphold. *She* set me up with the expectation for absolute perfection in myself and also made it so that other people came to expect the Good Girl out of me all the time as well."

"The Good Girl was a façade that I maintained to protect myself from vulnerability, judgment, and con- demnation…"

I paused, my pulse racing, as I tried to articulate this new truth. Amanda just nodded, and waited for me to continue.

"She also set the stage for the Good Girl to be expected in other females too, especially the little one running around my house that calls me mommy. But most of all, the Good Girl did a great job of creating a barrier of lies between me and God because she convinced me that she was all a part of Him, which was nothing but a lie. I guess, for me to really move forward and walk in joy, I have to start fresh and redefine what it means to truly be a *Good Girl*, according to God, not according to my parents, family, church, or even myself. I have to see, through His eyes, that what He called me to be is so much better than the Good Girl could have ever been. Her 'goodness' was rooted in guilt and fear, but what He really wants is for my true good character to flow freely out of His love for me and the joy that He gives."

"That's beautiful, Marlia." Amanda had tears in her eyes.

"Yes, it is! I can see now that God wants to literally break the expectations of perfectionism and release the bonds of the Good Girl. He's been trying to show me that the white picket fence that I searched for didn't really exist at all!"

I had finally realized that the false expectations and lying assumptions that I used to define God's character were also used as weapons of mass destruction against my own spirit and those around me.

Good Girl Impact

"Momma, I finished my letter to Santa!"

Savannah ran into my office waving her hand-printed letter high above her head, thrilled to show me what she had done. As she gave it to me, she quickly pointed out the picture that she had drawn for Santa to go along with her wish list.

Seeing the paper covered in a colorful rainbow and hearts sprinkled throughout, I oohed and aahed over what she had created, "Oh, baby, he is going to love your artwork! Since we need to practice, why don't you read me what you wrote."

Looking up at me with beaming eyes, she took the paper, cleared her throat, straightened her back, and began, "Dear Santa, I have been really helpful this year to my mommy and daddy and I've done really good in school..." She paused as she glanced up with a smile, which I returned with a nod of agreement. She continued on, "I have been a good girl all year, so please, can I have...?" as soon as she said the words, my heart dropped and started beating fast. I continued to smile at her with encouragement, but inside, I screamed at myself.

Look what you have done! She thinks that she has to be a good girl to get good things too! Oh, sweet Jesus, how do I right what I've so badly wronged! I'm not even sure that I know how...

"My sweet little girl," I started as I wrapped my arms around her and let the tear fall down my cheek.

What can I say to undo this?

The only words I could find were the ones my Father had said to me not long before, "My sweet little girl. You don't have to be a good girl, or perfect all of the time, to get what you want. You are already a good girl — *my girl* — worthy of every good and perfect gift. You're going to mess up, but that will never change my love for you."

She hugged me back, and then took off to put her letter in an envelope.

Sweet baby girl, we are going to figure this Good Girl thing out together.

The "Death" of the Good Girl?

Two weeks later, I was pushing against the deadline for the book, chain-chewing gum and eating way more pretzels than necessary.

Come on, Marlia! You gotta get this done. Only a few more days! If you don't do this in time…

Four hours passed, and I was still struggling to finish the section I was working on when, obviously sensing my stress, Amanda asked, "Marlia, are you okay? What's happening?"

"I'm stuck, and I'm worried that I'm not going to make the deadline."

"What happens if you don't?"

"Then I'm not doing what I'm supposed to be doing. I'm going to disappoint my family. I'm going to feel embarrassed. I'm…" as the next

As soon as she said the words, my heart dropped and I screamed at myself, Look at what you have done!

words crossed my mind, I looked up at her wide-eyed, "I'm not a *good girl* if I don't get it done."

She smiled that stupid smile, like she had been waiting for me to get there.

"Amanda! I'm still operating on the 'good girls get good things' belief!"

She nodded and waited.

"Can I kill her?" I smiled, but was only half-joking.

"How do I get rid of the Good Girl? She is ruining my life, setting me (and now Savannah!) up for stress and disillusionment. What am I going to do?"

"What *can* you do?"

"Can I kill her?" I smiled, but was only half-joking. This Good Girl-Matrix belief system had utterly messed up my life for more than three decades, and I wanted it over…done…finished.

"Do you really want to kill her?"

"I don't know." Something didn't feel right about the idea.

"What if there is another way? What does the Good Girl in you need right now in order to relax and allow God to be the Good Father, even if it makes her have to relinquish her Good Girl title? Even if she doesn't meet her own expectations or her family's? What does she need? What did you need, Marlia, when you were trying so desperately to be the Good Girl?"

"I needed to know that I would be loved, even if I messed up." I shook my head as the truth hit me with force.

Here I was about to kill her, when God just wants to love and redeem her... God, I have no idea how to do that, but I trust You will show me.

Chapter 5

Who Needs a Fence Anyway?

And yet this I call to mind
and therefore I have hope:
Because of the Lord's
great love we are not consumed,
for his compassions never fail.
They are new every morning;
great is your faithfulness.
I say to myself,
"The Lord is my portion;
therefore I will wait for him."
The Lord is good to those
whose hope is in him,
to the one who seeks him;
it is good to wait quietly
for the salvation of the Lord.
-Lamentations 3:21-26

I stood behind the pulpit and drew in a deep breath, trying to calm my nerves. It had been six long years since I had preached, taught, or even spoken to a group of people out of the Word of God. In those six years, my life had drastically changed, my family had been to the edge and back, and God had become *really* real. I was extremely anxious standing in this familiar place. This was the last pulpit that I spoke in before I left the ministry, painfully broken, and it was to be the first and very same one God would use in my re-entry. Truly, the irony of the situation was not lost on me, and I struggled not to chuckle out loud at God's sense of humor.

I shuffled my notes in front of me, taking great care that they stayed in order, steadied myself, and then looked up to the congregation with a nervous smile. For a split second, the glare of the bright lights caused me to flash back to the steaming hot tub, sitting under the black umbrella, raging at God and my circumstance.

My mom had sat across from me, neck deep in hot water, with tears in her eyes. Her baby girl was hurting...and so was she. After a long quiet moment, she broke her silence. "You know this isn't typical for me, but God told me something that He wants me to share with you."

Not giving me a chance to respond or gripe at her, she continued with an emotional thickness in her voice, "He said that you are lost and have walked away from your First Love. Marlia, you need to get back to it, to Him. I'm scared for you..."

As I refocused my eyes on the audience that was waiting for me to begin, I could feel the smile on my face grow, and become authentic.

I have found my First Love again.

I was on my way back from being lost. I was fully present and right where I was supposed to be —and it felt amazing. I asked the people to bow their heads with me, opened my mouth, and began to pray in preparation for our time together.

> *I finally felt completely present, like I was standing in the most "Marlia-ness" that I had ever experienced.*

And then…I almost lost myself in what God was doing in that sanctuary and in me. The next 45 minutes were surreal. As I spoke about the journey that God had led me on, and what He had shown me about Himself, I finally felt completely present, like I was standing in the most "Marlia-ness" that I had ever experienced. I was in the absolute essence that God created me to be, absent of ego and pride, purely an open vessel that the Holy Spirit was pouring into and through. It was so heavy that it made my head swirl.

As I finished, I looked out into the bright lights again and wondered, *How is it possible to feel so much joy? I still have my health issues; I'm still not even close to having all the answers; my life is still far from perfect; I'm still struggling with areas of disillusionment; I'm still looking for answers to why I ended up in this mess I'm in…so why the joy?*

Just a Little Taste of Yummy Joy

The joy I felt that day wasn't the result of my health problems disappearing, or me figuring it all out, or me realizing my life was perfect. In fact, as I stood in that pulpit in front of the congregation, I was still really struggling with areas of disillusionment.

This speaking opportunity occurred only one year after I was out of the hospital the first time, when I was still trying to figure out if God was really a Good Father. The bit of joy that God blessed me with that day came from finally feeling a moment of freedom from everything that weighed me down, from finally getting a glimpse of what the future could be like, from simply feeling blessed to be in that place, in that moment. It was just enough to make me hungrier for what I could have, and what He wanted to pour out on me as His gift of love. It was just a little taste, and I wanted more.

The next taste had come with the "aha" moment about the lie of the God-Matrix in the breakthrough coaching session that day, the redemption of the Good Girl, and the opportunity to see others through His eyes. And then came the sweet intimacy of dialogue opening up again between me and my Good Father.

I finally felt like I was approaching the end of this journey…that the joy He had promised was just around the corner.

My Own Lamentation?

As I finished looking over the outline for the book, it seemed like there was one more step in the process, but I couldn't see it. Frustrated, I shut down the computer and decided that I needed a little conversation with God to see if we could work it out.

"God, I really need direction for what You want next. I feel like I'm in over my head, and I need Your help. Amanda said I would probably write myself into my last chapter, so what is the last step to living in joy?"

As I began reading through the article, I couldn't help but laugh at what God had done.

I opened up my Bible, hoping the answer might jump off one of the pages as I flipped through.

"Lamentations 3," He answered.

"Uh, Lamentations 3…okay." I turned the pages until I found it. As I read, it felt strangely familiar. The emotion, the words, the process, so many of the verses resonated with my experience — as if I had lived them. My immediate instinct was to research, to find the backstory, to figure out why I identified so closely. Pulling it up on the Internet, the headline for a site about halfway down the page intrigued me: "The 5 Elements or Steps to a Lamentation."

As I began reading through the article, I couldn't help but laugh at what God had done. He had led me through writing my own

Lamentation. The first four steps that He had given me to walking in joy for the book lined up with the first four elements of the Biblical Lamentation!

I read them out loud again, just to make sure that I had understood them correctly, "Element #1 — Cry to God. Okay, so that lines up with the rage in the hot tub and the emotional expectations that set me up for disillusionment."

My excitement built as I continued, "Element #2 — Defining the Crisis/Complaint. Yep, that was my learning to submit to my "What Is," while making sure God knew that I wasn't happy about it. Element #3 — Asking God to Deliver and Give a Remedy. That definitely aligns with mourning the "What Was" and asking him to bring back normalcy. Element #4 — Statement of Confidence in God. Yes, yes, that was when I became sure that He is my Good Father by uncovering the lies of the 'God-Matrix.'"

What is the fifth step? I have to know!

As I read the final element, #5 — The Vow to Praise God, I found myself wanting to jump up and down, "This is the 'And Yet!!! The joy of Chapter 5!!!"

I shouted as I skipped around my office, "I finished it! I did it!"

Or did I?

Seriously, an Opportunity for Joy?

"There you go, Marlia. You're all set." The dialysis technician had just finished getting me set up for my three and a half hour session as I pulled out my laptop. I let out a deep sigh as I checked the clock, realizing that the majority of my day would be gone by the time I was done and out the door. I looked around the room at the other patients, some sleeping, some watching the little TVs that hung over each chair.

I wonder how long they have been doing this? How frustrated they get?

It had only been about ten months since the first treatment, but it felt like years because these days seemed to just drag by.

I should be out networking or going to a mom's group, or exercising, or...

I know this keeps me alive, so I can't complain, but it sure is inconvenient.

As I looked down at the two needles in my arm, I felt a rush of frustration.

I should be out networking, or going to a mom's group, or exercising, or grocery shopping. Mercy, I'd even take doing laundry — anything! — over being stuck to this machine three times a week! I can't even go on "vacation" for more than two days without reserving a seat at another clinic! And what about the impact on Savannah? She has to go to daycare because I can't be there to take care of her myself! This is keeping me from being the good mom and wife I should be! It's so messed up!

As I turned on my computer to pour my exasperation into the pages of my book, my cell phone rang.

"Hey Marlia, how's it going?" my friend chimed.

"Eh, it's alright. I'm sitting in dialysis, which is always a joy." My voice dripped with sarcasm.

"What do you do while you're there? Read? Sleep?"

"No, not really. Most of the time, I work on my book," I responded, trying not to sound too frustrated.

"Wow, that's really smart. I'm sure it's not the most fun thing, but at least you're being productive." She tried to encourage me, sensing that I was in a funk.

"Yeah, I guess. I would obviously rather be working on it at home because it's just such a pain to do it here."

"Sure, but would you actually take the time to write? I hate to say it, but what if this is a gift because it's forcing you to be still and do what God has called you to?"

I caught my breath, trying to find the words. "Yeah, I guess you're right," was all I could say.

When we hung up, I laid my head back against the chair and closed my eyes.

She's right about it forcing me to be still. Maybe the Good Girl in me would have kept me too busy running around, trying to keep everything perfect for my family, my church, and everyone else, leaving me no time to do what He has asked me to do. Maybe this is a gift — a way for God to finally get me back to joy.

The Voice of the Good Girl

It had already been a long day, and it was only noon. Our heads spun after Josh and I finished three hours of nutrition, financial, and insurance classes in the first part of the morning, all with the apparent goal of discouraging us from moving forward. Now we sat and waited in another chilled, stark white room for the surgeon to come in and give me the once over. While Josh played on his cell phone, I thought back to eighteen months earlier when we sat in that very same room, waiting for the very same surgeon, only to be disappointed again.

We had walked in hoping to hear him say I was a perfect candidate for a kidney transplant. And he did say that. But then he had finished with, "…except for your weight. You will need to lose about 50 pounds before we can proceed with testing your donors."

Are you flippin' kidding me??? My weight??? Of course it's my weight!!!

My weight had been an issue that I had struggled with since childhood, and even though I tried to eat clean and maintain a strict kidney diet, it was still the bane of my adulthood.

I tried not to sound sarcastic or angry when I asked him how I was supposed to do that while taking a pile of pills that were notorious for making weight loss extremely difficult.

"You're going to need to only eat about 700-900 calories a day and exercise for two hours, six days a week."

Oh, is that all? I can barely walk a flight of stairs, and you want me to work out? Feeling nothing but fury, I decided it was better not to share what I was thinking.

"Once you do that, give us a call again, and we'll see if we can get the process started for you."

Frustration, anger, and hopelessness took over, and it took me eighteen months to lose the 50 pounds and find the courage to walk back into that doctor's office.

I've worked hard and lost the weight, but will something else come up now?

I paused as that last question crossed my mind and realized that I was hearing the voice of the Good Girl this time.

For crying out loud, I'm already disillusioned, and I haven't heard the doctor say a thing yet!

The Good Girl continued, *Will I ever be healed? Will I ever run with my little girl again? Will Josh ever be able to exhale, and stop worrying when the next shoe is going to drop? Will my life ever not revolve around doctor's appointments and medications? Will I ever be whole again? Will I ever be able to do what I'm supposed to be doing and be who I am supposed to be being?*

Josh could tell that I was nervous and tried to steady me by squeezing my hand. I looked over and smiled just as the doctor walked through the door with what I hoped was good news.

"It's good to see you again, Mrs. Cochran."

That's it! I'm going to get my life back again!

"It's good to see you too." I began to shake a bit and hoped it wasn't evident in my voice.

"Well, congratulations on losing the weight! You've done exactly what we asked of you, which will make the recovery much easier for you. Everything else is looking good so far, so we'd like to start in-depth testing on you. How does that sound?"*

"Um, that sounds awesome!" I wanted to puke and jump up and down at the same time.

Oh my gosh! It's really gonna happen!

"So once we get the testing done on you, and get an approval from the surgeon committee to proceed, we can start testing your willing donors. If one of them matches, we can actually do this within three to six months. If they don't match, you'll be on the list, which could take up to eight to ten years. But let's hope for the best, eh?"

---

*Because people have asked for information regarding how I lost the weight and my overall journey towards health, I've included a Resource section at the end of the book.

"Yes, thank you doctor." I shot a side smile to Josh as we got up to leave, trying to not jump up and down and act a fool with excitement.

That's it! I'm going to get my life back again! I'll be able to run, and work, and play, and everything will be back to normal! Everything is going to be better as soon as this happens! I can't wait!

I paused. *There she goes again! Wait a minute, Good Girl.*

I took a deep breath, remembering that my intention was to redeem her, and asked myself what my Good Girl needed to hear at that moment to relax.

Everything is in God's hands. We are going to be okay, maybe even find some joy, regardless of the outcome.

I knew it was easier said than done, as I'd spent many years with this Good Girl running the show, so I asked for help as I opened the car door and slid in to my seat.

Please, please, please, Jesus…work this all out. You know how much I want this, but I want what You want more. Help me to focus on You and Your timing and remember that You are My Good Father. I can trust you…and somehow find joy in the process…regardless of what happens.

I'm glad I asked because, once again, life was not going to go as planned…

Back at the Beginning?

It seemed to be the week from hell...literally. I'm not one to find the devil behind every bush, but it sure felt like he was trying to break me around every turn. Highly aggravated, I sat at my desk attempting to pull together the dozens of forms required for the testing to get my kidney transplant. I had worked feverishly toward this for more than a year, and it still just wasn't coming easily. As I flipped through the pages, I realized that I had filled most of them out incorrectly, and in a flash of frustrated anger, I threw them all up in the air, making it rain sheets of white all around me.

I slumped forward and dropped my head on the desk in front of me, drawing in deep breaths through my nose and pushing them out through my mouth, attempting to calm my rapidly climbing blood pressure.

Abba, if I wasn't sick, I wouldn't have to deal with this. If you would just heal me, I could serve you so much more easily. Why does it have to be so hard?

As I tried to focus my breathing, a conversation from the day before with Savannah's teacher, that didn't quite go as anticipated, flooded into my mind. "Mr. and Mrs. Cochran, I just want you to know that I love having Savannah in my class. She is such an amazing girl, with a gentle and kind heart, who tries to be so helpful. She truly is a joy." With proud smiles, we both nodded our heads in agreement, glad that her new teacher was so fond of our girl. "That being said, I'm concerned because it seems like she is really struggling to progress or even keep up. I think that we may want to consider putting her in a lower level class so that she doesn't get frustrated and give up."

I could feel the flush of heat start at the top of my head and race down to the tip of my feet. Exasperated, I gripped Josh's hand more tightly, "But how did it change so much from last year? Why is there such a disparity?" As tears formed in my eyes, I could see them form in her teacher's as well.

"I think that the tests last year might have been slanted a bit, not graded as strictly as they should have been. Because her teacher loved her so much, she just couldn't see the truth."

As sweet as her "now" teacher was, as amazing as her "then" teacher had been, I had this overwhelming urge to punch them both in the throat as the crazy mom raged inside me, even though it wasn't their fault.

"I love having Savannah in my class, and I'm concerned because it seems she's really struggling..."

"I'm sorry that it isn't the news you were hoping to hear, but we will work our hardest with her. We just want to make sure that she does the best *she* can do, and not break her spirit in the process."

As her teacher continued to reassure us, the anger subsided into sorrow for the journey that my sweet girl had walked already and would continue in. I couldn't help in that moment but reach up to my Father.

God, didn't we already do this? I thought we were moving past it all. Please help her. Help us. Protect her spirit above everything else.

With that memory so fresh from the day before, my tears puddled on the desk. I struggled with confusion as to why God wouldn't just heal us both. Just make it all better, so that she wouldn't have to experience the frustration of trying so hard without the results or deal with mean kids and their ignorant words. Just a quick touch, causing my kidneys and body to function as it should so there wouldn't be any more needles, medicines, or thoughts as to what the future may, or may not, hold.

God, didn't we already do this? I thought we were moving past it all.

God, seriously, haven't we had enough? It feels like we're back at the beginning all over again. Where is the joy in this? When will it stop being so hard?

"Marlia, the joy is in the 'and yet.' My sweet girl, joy is not a place you will arrive one day when all of the suffering ends, and the problems disappear. Those are a part of the human experience, and they give you the opportunity to choose — even feel — joy, regardless of circumstance or situation. Can you choose to say, and live, and breathe 'And yet I will praise Him,' even if you have to be on dialysis for the rest of your life? Even if Savannah never catches up? No matter what?"

I will try, Abba. I'm choosing it right now, but I don't feel it, and I'm not sure how to do that. But I'm willing. Show me…guide me into the 'and yet'….

Do I Really Believe?

"Amanda, I'm struggling with the book. I'm still scared I won't finish it in time for the event."

She sat across from me, red pen in one hand and tea in the other. We had met at Starbucks to work on edits for the completed chapters.

She looked up from the papers laid out in front of her, "What if you don't?"

"Yeah, that's not even an option. I *have* to finish it. I've told everyone that I would. I would just look stupid." I couldn't even entertain the idea of not making the deadline without feeling like I was going to throw up.

Making eye contact to really get her point across, she asked a question that stopped me dead in my tracks: "What if God isn't done with it yet? What if He's not done showing you how to walk in joy regardless of the situation?"

Not wanting to hear that, or think it could be a possibility, I looked away, shifting in my chair.

When I didn't answer, she continued, "Would you be able to still have joy, to still be joyful, even if your book didn't come out when you were hoping it would? Would you be able to walk your own process? Or would you be stuck in disillusionment? This is it, Marlia — where the rubber meets the road."

So this is what the "and yet" is really all about. Man, I hope I can get this to my heart sooner than later!

Well, the rubber really did meet the road at my next opportunity to speak to a moms' group, when my Good Girl faced an ultimate challenge.

Redeeming the Good Girl

I sat in front of my computer, notes and Bible spread out in front of me, at my wits' end. I looked up at the clock, feeling frantic. I had literally been in the same position for ten hours, and still nothing. No direction, no outline, no solid points that I could even try to muddle through.

Oh my gosh! I'm going to stand up in front of those women tomorrow morning and BLOW IT!

I folded my arms on my desk and laid my head down on them, partially out of exhaustion, but mostly out of exasperation.

Seriously, God, this never happens to me! I never struggle to figure out what I'm going to say. Can you toss me a bone here?!?!?

Wracking my brain in an attempt to pull two thoughts together, I heard Him say, "Just get up there and do it."

Stunned and appalled, my Good Girl shot back, "Without notes?"

"Yes."

"Yeah, that's just ludicrous. How can I possibly get up in front of these moms without notes, without an outline, and tell my story...FOR AN HOUR?"

Still calm and steady, He repeated, "Just get up there and do it."

"Man, You are really pushin' my buttons. What if I get up there and mess it all up? What if I run out of stuff to say? What if I fall flat on my face? I will be so humiliated! They'll never ask me back again!" My heart was beating so hard that I could feel it in my throat. I knew what He was asking me to do, and it scared me to death.

"Marlia, just get up there and do it. Trust Me."

Shaking at the prospect, my Good Girl and I relinquished. "So I guess I'm going to get up there and just do it. I really hope You show up for this one."

"Man, You are really pushin' my buttons. What if I get up there and mess it all up?"

The next morning, I wanted to throw up as the group leader introduced me, and the applause called me to move toward the stage. My hands were sweating so bad that I was afraid to take the microphone for fear of dropping it. I set my Bible down on the podium along with a one-page security blanket of random thoughts that didn't even go together. Looking out at the ladies that sat before me, I smiled nervously, trying to make eye contact with them to get a feel for what they needed, in hopes that something would come.

"Let's start our time off together with prayer." As we all bowed our heads, I heard God whisper into my spirit, "Remember, just get up here and do it."

As I wrapped up the prayer, I looked down at my lame attempt at notes and knew right then that I wasn't going to use them, because this is where the rubber was gonna meet the road.

"Ladies, I need you to hold me accountable today. This is going to be the very first time that I ever speak to a group with true authenticity. I need you to help me stay transparent because this is the first time that I'm going to speak without my Good Girl pants on."

I picked up my black umbrella, popped it open, and began, "I sat under this black umbrella in my hot tub everyday for a year, screaming and raging at God because I believed He had abandoned me..."

As I told my story — my journey with God — the words just poured out. The more that I spoke from a place of truth, without the Good Girl façade that I always had before, the more that God showed up in that room. He gave me the courage to share parts of my story I had never before publicly shared. As I looked out over the group, I could see the tears streaming and the heads nodding.

I can almost physically see God using my story to heal their hearts!

I was floored, almost overcome, with what I was witnessing…what I was participating in.

This is so much more beautiful than anything I could have imagined, let alone planned.

As I closed our time in prayer, I glanced at the clock and realized that it had been exactly one hour…and I didn't use my notes once.

Thank you for being My Good Father — for showing up for me and for these women. When can we do it again?

This is Joy

Three weeks later, I sat in the circle with the women who had walked this book journey with me. When it was my turn to update the group on my progress, I felt something I hadn't felt in the entire eighteen months I'd been with them…

"Well, the book isn't finished, and we have less than five weeks to get it done, designed, and published for the event. I'm in the deep end of kidney transplant paperwork and testing, and it's all uncertain. And, some of my friends and family are not giving me the type of support I'd hoped they would give me for the completion of my book…"

I paused, letting the Good Girl's frustration, fear, and disappointment come up. I knew that my disillusionment with the situations and the people in my life were just the result of expectations — the White Picket Fence illusion that had been created by a culture that doesn't know how to deal with things not being a certain way. And I'd learned to stop holding my breath, and pushing down the tears, and pasting that silly smile on my face.

It's better to feel it…to be real about it…

> "*I am His girl, and that's enough.*"

"But I know that my Good Father has a perfect plan for me. I know that I don't have to be a Good Girl for Him to give me good things. I am *His girl,* and that's enough. I know that even if the kidney transplant doesn't work out…even if Savannah never catches up…even if this flippin' book doesn't get done in time for the event…and even if my loved ones don't come around with the support I desire…it will all be good…"

And then It happened…I realized it already was…

"Ladies, I don't know that I even have words for what's been happening. Seeing God show up for me and those women at the moms' group…it was…" I struggled through grateful tears before continuing, "…it was so incredible. I just want to do it again. I just want God to use me…that way. It made the whole journey worth it. Not just the last eighteen months of uncovering the lies of the God-Matrix and the Good Girl-Matrix, but all of it. The crazy boyfriend, the brush with death, the infertility, the dialysis, all of it…all of the disillusionment. God redeemed my story that day. He redeemed my Good Girl…"

Another deep breath that I felt go to the core of my being, all the way to the deepest part of my spirit, gave way to what I'd always craved…

"I think I'm actually…finally…feeling it…I am walking in JOY!"

About Marlia

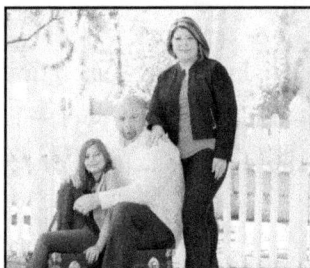

Transformational Speaker and Author Marlia Cochran founded Good Girl Enterprises to help women of all ages to walk the journey from disillusionment to the joy God has promised His children.

While receiving her BA Degree in Christian Ministry with a Minor in Psychology (Azusa Pacific University) and a MA in Pastoral Studies with a Youth Ministry Emphasis (Haggard Graduate School of Theology, APU), she passionately pursued God's call to serve students and their families as a Youth Pastor for 10 years. However, while continuing her education for a Masters of Divinity, Marlia found herself facing a health crisis that nearly killed her *and* her faith. Disillusioned and raging, she sunk deeper and deeper, until she finally surrendered at death's doorstep. Even after a miraculous healing, Marlia found herself disconnected and depressed, questioning God's goodness, and asking Him to restore her "White Picket Fence." The journey He took her on over the next few years not only answered all of her questions in the most surprising way possible, it gave her access to what she had really always wanted: His Joy.

And now, Marlia is helping other women find that Joy and take it back into their communities. She is also the co-host of Elevate4Women Radio (facebook.com/elevate4women).

Marlia currently resides in Southern California with her best friend and husband Josh, her sweet daughter Savannah, and their dog Princess Kiatta. She loves spending time with her family, cuddling up in front of a good movie, photographing whatever finds its way in front of her lens, and trying out new recipes she discovers on Pinterest.

Contact Marlia at:
Info@GoodGirlEnterprises.com
or
Facebook.com/GoodGirlEnterprises

Good Girl Enterprises

W hat I've realized over the past two years is that this journey — of walking in joy and redeeming the Good Girl — is not one to be walked alone.

Good Girl Enterprises is a Spirit-led transformational coaching and training company that God called me to establish for this reason…so that you don't have to walk it alone either.

If you want to uncover your God-Matrix and redeem your Good Girl, if you're ready to walk in the full joy that your Good Father has promised, then I want to invite you to download this FREE Tele-class audio recording:

Where's My White Picket Fence? — Part 1 of 3

In this 60-minute audio, we will begin to unpack and identify the false expectations that keep us trapped in disillusionment, pain, and anger.

To receive your FREE Tele-class,
go to the website below and click on the
Where's My White Picket Fence?
offer on the right side of the page:
www.GoodGirlEnterprises.com

For specific questions and requests for coaching, retreats,
or other opportunities, please contact me at:
Info@GoodGirlEnterprises.com

Resources

Health

The National Kidney Foundation
www.Kidney.org

Vasculitis Foundation
www.VasculitisFoundation.org

Visalus Sciences / Body By Vi
www.JoshCochran.MyVi.com

Book/Message & Author Transformation

Amanda Johnson
True To Intention
www.TrueToIntention.com

Spiritual Transformation

Pastor Tami
www.PastorTamiMinistries.com

Azusa House of Prayer
www.azhop.org

Blue Letter Bible
www.BlueLetterBible.org